Yorkshire Dales

Colin Speakman

original photography by
Alex Ramsay

HarperCollins*Publishers*

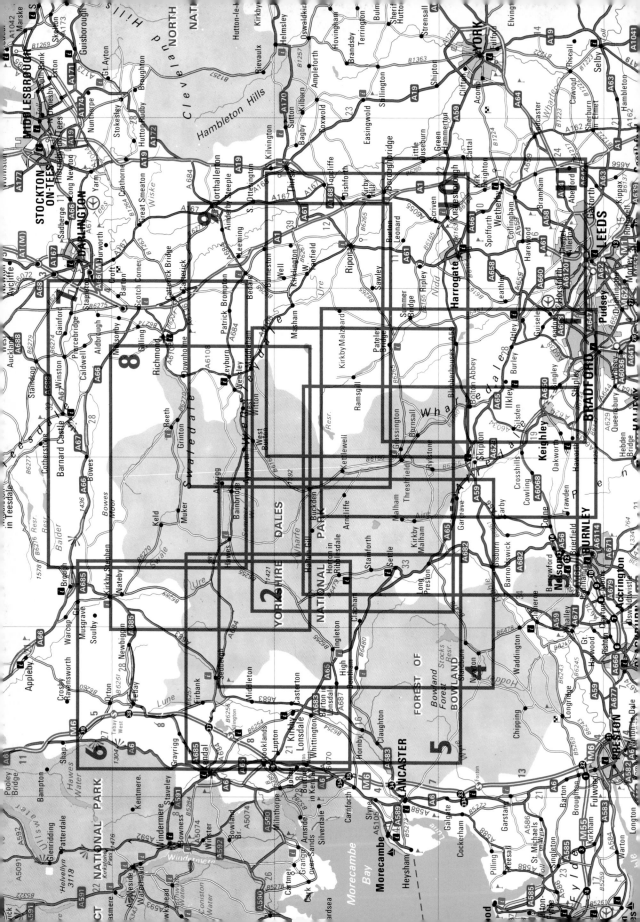

CONTENTS

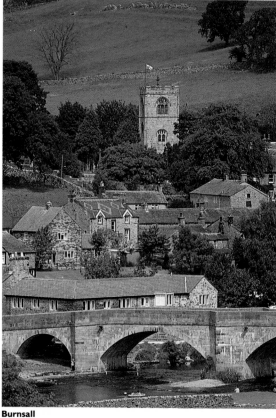

Burnsall

The Strid, River Wharfe

Preceding page: **Bolton Priory**

Wharfedale from below Beamsley Beacon

Most people from this region of the country will tell you that Ilkley is where true Yorkshire Dales country begins. As you travel north-westwards from the towns and cities of West Yorkshire, you will immediately notice a fairly dramatic change in the scenery. The landscape becomes increasingly enclosed – the heather-covered moors rise up above the green pastureland and scattered woods to form long, high horizons that seem almost to meet the clouds.

'Dale' to the local inhabitants means rather more than just a mere valley. A dale is everything

Grimwith Reservoir

Barden Tower

that lies within those long lines of empty, smooth-topped fells. A dale is a community, a tiny self-contained kingdom along which people travel to meet their neighbours 'up' and 'down' dale; rarely will the local people venture over the steep moorland passes into the unfamiliar territory of the next valley.

Wharfedale is the longest and perhaps the grandest of the Yorkshire Dales. It is a meandering, twisting valley of astonishing beauty and variety. The River Wharfe, which runs the whole length of Wharfedale, has its source as a moorland stream almost 2000 feet (610 m) above sea level on Cam Fell; it runs through Wharfedale down to where it sluggishly sweeps into the River Ouse at Cawood, south of York. There are three common ways of travelling through Wharfedale. You can drive through it, cycle through it, or best of all walk along it; there is no way better than along the Dales Way, an 81-mile (130 km) long footpath which follows the banks of the river from Ilkley, in Mid Wharfedale, and continuing on as far as Bowness-on-Windermere in the Lake District. Of course you don't have to walk the entire length of the footpath to get a good feel for this magnificent scenery.

Wharfedale

Packhorse bridge, Ilkley

Ilkley Moor (SW)

View of Ilkley from White Wells, Ilkley Moor (SW)

Woods near Bolton Priory

Looking across to Simon's Seat, Barden Fell (SW)

In Mid Wharfedale the Wharfe is still a mountain river, broad and shallow, but peat brown in colour, and capable of rising at immense speed. The Romans named a local Goddess after it – Verbeia. She was known for her treachery as well as her beauty, and she demanded regular gifts – no doubt to prevent supplicants from suddenly being swept from their horses over the slippery ford. The ford still exists and can be seen behind the site of the Roman fort at Ilkley.

This is a landscape, which over the centuries, has provided pleasure for people in a variety of ways. Ilkley, for example, was famed as a spa in the last century, becoming incredibly popular and fashionable for the rich and well-to-do whether they suffered from serious ailments or not. Its crisp moorland air and walks were valued as much as its health-giving springs. But the moors above and around Bolton Abbey, Barden and Burnsall were, for centuries, a hunting ground for the medieval Lords of Skipton Castle and their successors, the Dukes of Devonshire. The latter turned the uplands first of all into a vast deer forest to hunt the native red deer, and in later years to some of the finest grouse shooting moors in all England. The seemingly natural expanse of richly purple heather is the result of careful management of the moorland as a breeding ground for black and red grouse to accommodate the increasingly popular sport of grouse shooting.

This area now forms one of the most popular and most visited parts of the Yorkshire Dales National Park.

In Britain, National Parks are neither nationally owned nor are they 'parks' in the usual sense of the word. They are areas which are nationally important for their landscape and wildlife heritage, yet more often than not privately owned, farmed or forested. The public has no more rights within them than elsewhere in Britain.

National Parks are, however, given special protection and finance by central government through the means of a National Park Authority. These bodies have the twin duties of conserving natural beauty and of encouraging its enjoyment by the public – requirements that often have to be very carefully balanced if areas like the Yorkshire Dales are not to be swamped by too many visitors, their cars and all the other trimmings that often accompany areas popular with tourists.

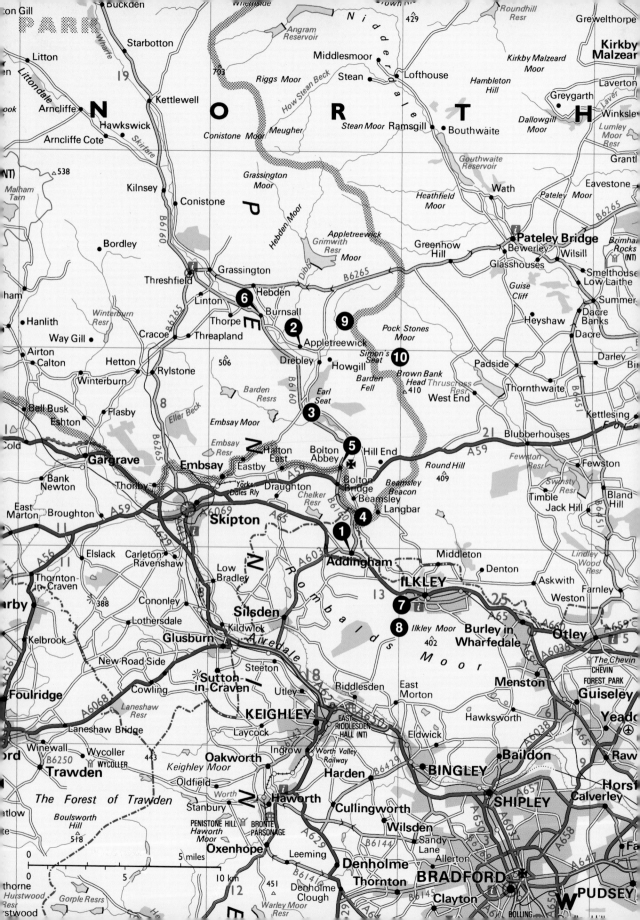

❶ ADDINGHAM

Addingham village, near the banks of the Wharfe, has a medieval church close to an extensive village green. The village has some remarkable, early Industrial Revolution cottages and old textile mills; most, however, have now been converted for other uses. A footpath crosses the Wharfe by a little suspension bridge and climbs to the summit of Beamsley Beacon (1300 ft/393 m), a great moorland ridge and superb viewpoint.

❷ APPLETREEWICK

Appletreewick, once famous for its medieval Onion Fair, is a pretty, one-street village. The Fair is recalled by a green track, still known as Onion Lane, which leads down to the River Wharfe, where bunches of onions were hung for sale. Several of the cottages date from the 17th century or earlier.

❸ BARDEN TOWER

Barden Tower is the ruin of a great medieval hunting lodge where Lord Henry Clifford (1463–1523) once lived. He was one of the famous Cliffords of Skipton Castle who, after his father was slain during the Wars of the Roses, grew up in hiding before his estates were restored in 1485. He was taught philosophy and astronomy by the monks of Bolton Priory. He remained a man widely respected for his goodness, wisdom and simple habits but who also, in 1513, fought against the Scots at Flodden Field.

❹ BEAMSLEY

Beamsley is a quiet village notable for Beamsley Hospital, which lies about half a mile from the village. It is an unusual circular almshouse, built in the mid 17th century by Lady Anne Clifford to house the poor of the parish. The building with its chapel and tiny garden is open to the public most days of the year.

❺ BOLTON ABBEY AND STRID WOODS

Bolton Abbey village gets its name from Bolton Priory, a collection of ruins situated on a little headland above the River Wharfe. The Priory was established in the 12th century, and the church, which escaped destruction during the Dissolution, still serves the people of the village.

You can walk from the Priory through tranquil woods to the Cavendish Pavilion where refreshments are available. Continue into Strid Woods along a series of well-marked trails. These lead to the terrifying Strid, a ferocious white-water ravine through which the river plunges and where many have met their deaths trying to leap or 'stride' across.

❻ BURNSALL

Burnsall enjoys an almost perfect riverside setting between the high fells. There is an ancient bridge over the Wharfe, a church with Anglo-Viking gravestones and an inn hidden behind rambling roses. The 17th-century Grammar School was endowed by Sir William Craven, 'the Dick Whittington of the Dales', who was born in Appletreewick before leaving his native dale to become Lord Mayor of London (1610–12), and returning to become a benefactor of the village. Among easy walks from Burnsall are the fieldpath to Thorpe-in-the-Hollow or alternatively take the riverside paths down to Appletreewick or up river past Loup Scar to the little suspension bridge which leads to Hebden.

❼ ILKLEY

Originally an Iron-Age settlement, Ilkley later became a Roman camp guarding the shallow ford across the Wharfe where a network of military roads crossed the valley, branching to York, Boroughbridge or Bainbridge.

It was here, centuries later, that the healing properties of a moorland spring high up on Ilkley Moor were, according to local legend, discovered by a shepherd who had injured his leg and which later recovered after being bathed in the waters. The spring – known as White Wells – brought people from all over Britain during the late 18th century. They were carried up a steep path on the backs of donkeys to a tiny Bathhouse built around the spring. There they would immerse themselves in the ice cold waters as a means of curing gout and other conditions. White Wells, including one of the plunge baths, has been beautifully restored. Refreshments available (Open Easter–mid Oct Sats and Suns; Bank Hol afternoons)

The spa town itself has kept its original charm and style. Places to visit include the parish church with its rare Anglo-Viking crosses, an elegant main shopping street and the Tudor Manor House Art Gallery and Museum with displays of the town's long history from Roman times to the present-day. (Open Tues–Sun; Bank Hol Mon)
☏ 0943 602319

❽ ILKLEY MOOR

Many people walk from the centre of Ilkley through the streamside gardens along Wells Promenade and up to Ilkley Moor – a vast expanse of open heather moorland and rough grassland. Made famous by the folk song *On Ilkla Moor Baht 'At*, paths and tracks lead along and across the moor. It is an area rich in archaeological remains, including a stone circle known as the Twelve Apostles.

❾ PARCEVAL HALL

Parceval Hall, a restored Tudor mansion, is now a Church of England retreat. It has sheltered south-facing terraced gardens overlooking the little valley of Skyreholmefull. The gardens are beautifully kept and full of rare plants and shrubs. (Open Apr–Oct daily) Close by is the eerie limestone gorge of Trollers' Ghyll.

❿ SIMON SEAT

From Strid Woods you can walk through parkland of majestic oaks, past the waterfalls of the Valley of Desolation (its curiously inappropriate name recalling a 19th-century landslide) to the summit of Simon Seat (1550 ft/485 m), the gritstone crags of which form a high point known as Barden Fell. This is a popular ramble (8 miles/13 km) across the National Park Public Access Area (closed on shooting days and at times of high fire risk) to a magnificent viewpoint high above Wharfedale and the Skyreholme valley.

Upper Wharfedale

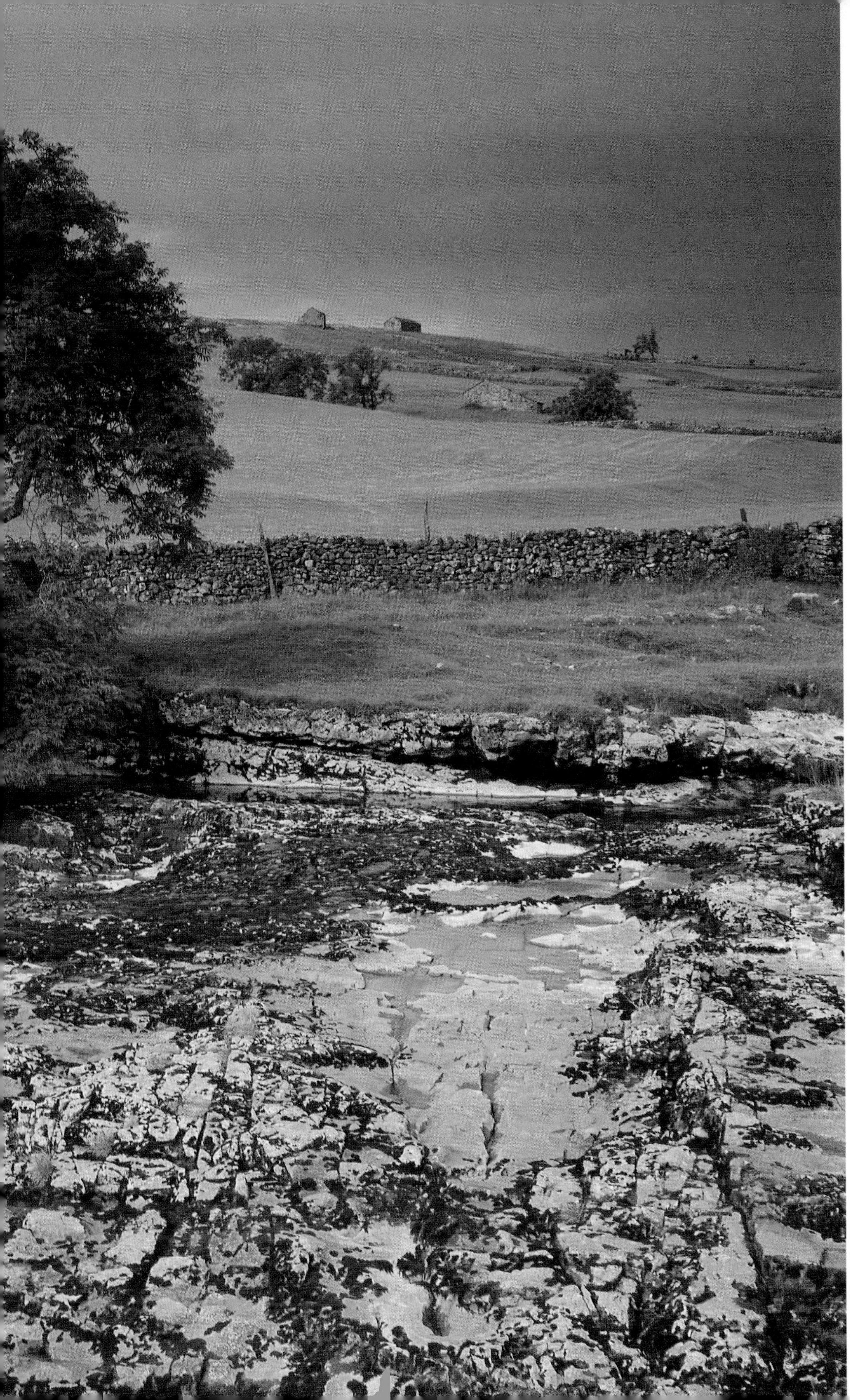

Preceding page: Langstrothdale

Arncliffe Church, Littondale (SW)

Littondale in winter (SW)

Kilnsey Crag

Litton (TC)

As you travel north of Burnsall, the scenery of Wharfedale changes dramatically. The reason for this lies in the limestone bedrock. For above Burnsall the heather-covered, dark gritstone moorlands, with their craggy summits, yield to a much softer and lighter landscape. The difference is perhaps most noticeable in the drystone walls, which in Mid Wharfedale are typically dark grey, but in Upper Wharfedale become light grey and can sometimes appear white in bright sunlight. Barns, farms and even cottages constructed of this attractive stone reflect these paler colours, while the pastures are lusher and greener thanks to the lime-rich soils that have developed here.

Only as you climb away from the terraced valley sides onto the open moorland summits, capped with sandstones, shales and grits, do you find yourself back onto the dark, acid moorlands. If you look carefully in areas where the two kinds

View across Wharfedale to Kilnsey Moor

of rock meet, the walls are speckled light and dark. The change of rock is caused by a long, and complex line of geological faulting, known as the Craven Fault. The fault is actually a great fracture in the Earth's surface allowing deeper, older rocks to be pushed towards the surface.

The Craven Fault begins in the area west of Ingleton and cuts right into the southern part of the Yorkshire Dales, actually splitting into three distinct fault lines known as the North, Mid and South Craven Faults. Even after millions of years of erosion these faults have left often dramatic effects on the landscape, such as exposed crags and rocky, scree-skirted scars which are a common feature of Malhamdale and Upper Wharfedale. Where the fault line crosses the river, as it does, for example, at Linton Falls near Grassington, an attractive series of waterfalls can often be seen.

Bridge at Hubberholme

Conistone (SW)

Grassington (SW)

Above Kettlewell

The complex geology of the region has created other interesting features. Around Burnsall, Thorpe, Linton and Cracoe are to be seen a series of smooth conical hills known as reef knolls. These are hillocks of almost pure limestone which evolved like vast coral reefs from primeval shallow seas.

Farther north the dale narrows and its sides steepen, having been scoured out by the action of ancient glaciers into a characteristic U-shaped valley. As you climb away from the riverside, you find yourself crossing a series of long narrow terraces of limestone, down which moorland streams have carved narrow, spectacularly beautiful side valleys or gills. There are small caves and areas of limestone pavement where the soil has been eroded away into free-standing 'clints' between deep crevices or 'grykes'.

The limestone terraces, especially where they are wooded, are rich in wild flowers once common in our meadows and uplands, but now rare — such as cowslips, violets, mountain pansies, primroses, the lovely bird's eye primrose, lilies of the valley and a variety of orchids, all now strictly protected by law. It is also an area rich in birdlife. Birds of prey hover over the

Old lead workings near Stump Cross Caverns (SW)

The River Wharfe

higher moorlands, seemingly motionless as they wait for the moment to fall on their prey. The species that you are most likely to see are hen harriers, kestrels, the occasional buzzard, as well as curlews and plovers, while herons, dippers and even the occasional kingfisher dart around the riverside.

North of Kilnsey, the dale splits, with Littondale bearing away to the west and Wharfedale continuing as far north as Buckden before also bearing north-westwards, leaving the main road to Wensleydale to ascend Kidstone Pass into Bishopdale. Moorland becks, high on Cam Fell, form the source of the River Wharfe. Here, close to its source, the Wharfe is little more than a fast moving stream, tumbling over rapids and little falls, as it twists its way through Langstrothdale, past small communities with Viking names, such as Hubberholme, Yockenthwaite and Oughtershaw.

As you follow the road up Langstrothdale, you will climb from the dalehead over the murderously steep pass of Fleet Moss into Hawes, leaving behind you the most untouched, and for this reason many people's favourite dale.

17

❶ ARNCLIFFE

An outstanding example of a former defensive settlement. The cottages are situated around the village green where the cattle could be easily gathered and where they and the community were better protected against marauding Scots.

❷ BUCKDEN

Buckden was once a deer hunting lodge at the edge of a Norman hunting reserve or 'Forest of Langstrothdale'. The National Park car park and Dalesbus terminus provide a good starting point for a choice of walks, either to Buckden Pike (1302 ft/702 m), perhaps the most impressive peak in Wharfedale, or past the hamlet of Cray and continuing beyond Cray Gill into Langstrothdale.

❸ CONISTONE

Conistone is an unspoiled stone-built village. A nearby footpath climbs up Conistone Dibb, a narrow limestone gorge; or else take the medieval trackway (still known as Scot Gate), which climbs over the desolate moors to Mossdale and Nidderdale.

❹ GRASSINGTON

In Grassington, the main town of Upper Wharfedale, tourism has replaced lead-mining as the main industry, and the former miners' cottages are now sought-after weekend retreats. It is a charming town, with plenty to see and do. A lively music festival takes place here every June and there is an art exhibition in the town hall during August. The National Park Centre can provide you with information on the area (Open Easter–Oct daily; winter Sat and Sun. Phone 0756 752748) The Upper Wharfedale Museum in the square has displays of dales' agriculture and mining. Refreshments available (Open afternoons Apr–Oct daily; Nov–Mar Sat and Sun. Phone 0756 752800) Pletts Barn, a magnificent 18th-century barn and dovecot outside which John Wesley once preached, is now an 'outdoor' shop and mountain-bike hire base, (Open daily. Phone 0756 752266) and a watercolour gallery upstairs (Phone 0756 753043)

Walks to be enjoyed pass by Linton Falls, the 12th-century Linton Church – 'the Cathedral of the Dales' – and Linton village itself, which, with its wide stream, 18th-century almshouse, white-walled pub and handsome cottages, is one of the most beautiful in the dale.

❺ GRIMWITH RESERVOIR

This large moorland reservoir is reached by a long drive off the main Grassington–Pateley road immediately to the north of Dibble's Bridge. There is a large car park and marked trails around the entire reservoir. Look out for a superbly restored ling (heather) thatched barn which dates back to pre-Dissolution times. At the west end of the reservoir is an important wildfowl sanctuary.

❻ HEBDEN

Hebden's farms and cottages crowd along a narrow tributary of the Wharfe, Hebden Gill. Like other villages, Hebden owes its existence to the extensive lead mines on the local moors which were worked from medieval times until late last century. The track from the village up the Gill passes a series of waterfalls to Yarnbury, where remains of this industry can be seen all year round, including the impressive smelt mill chimney and flues high on the moor.

❼ KETTLEWELL

Kettlewell is a delightful village situated where the steep, side-valley of Cam Beck meets the Wharfe. The village has no less than three inns, dating back to when this former lead-mining community was also an important coaching stop on stage-coach routes between Yorkshire and Teeside.

Kettlewell is the starting point of popular walks to the summit of Great Whernside (2310 ft/704 m) over into Littondale or along the riverside to the smaller village of Starbotton higher up the dale.

❽ KILNSEY

Kilnsey is overlooked by its huge, limestone crag, an overhang carved out by an ancient glacier. Its summit is the destination for the

Fell Race that forms part of the celebrated Kilnsey Show, held on the Tuesday after every August Bank holiday. Kilnsey was once an important Grange belonging to the monks of Fountains Abbey. A tiny fragment of the gatehouse of the Grange survives in front of the Jacobean Old Hall. Nearby, Kilnsey Trout Farm welcomes visitors to feed and buy fish and game. (Open all year daily. Phone 0756 752150)

❾ LANGSTROTHDALE

Through Langstrothdale, a sparkling little mountain river and road share a narrow valley running past farming communities that have retained their original Nordic names – the scattered farms of Yockenthwaite, for example, or Hubberholme with a church notable for its rare rood-loft screen to name two. Yet this deep pass between the hills is of even greater antiquity, as shown by a Bronze Age circle above Deepdale – close to the footpath but hidden behind a field wall.

❿ LITTONDALE

Littondale is a valley of exquisite, unspoiled beauty, with picturesque villages such as Arncliffe and Litton. From here take the spectacular mountain roads which climb across the watersheds to Malhamdale and Ribblesdale. In Ribblesdale, once a Norman hunting forest, lie tiny and remote hamlets such as Halton Gill and Cosh.

⓫ STUMP CROSS CAVERN

Stump Cross Craven, easily reached from Hebden by taking the spectacular Pateley Bridge road, is an impressive show cave. It was formed as the result of old mine workings opening into natural caverns. As well as beautifully lit galleries of stalactites and stalagmites, many of them with fanciful names, a small museum and exhibition area of local finds can be enjoyed in the visitor centre. Refreshments available (Open Apr–Oct daily; Nov–Mar, Sat and Sun) Major archaeological discoveries made at Stump Cross include the bones of animals no longer found in Britain, such as bear and wolverine.

Converted warehouses, Skipton

Kirkby Malham

Preceding page: Malhamdale   Yorkshire Day Procession, Skipton

Gritstone cottages, Skipton

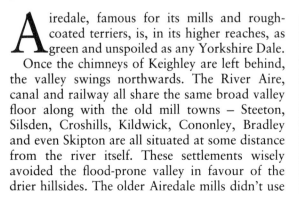

iredale, famous for its mills and rough-coated terriers, is, in its higher reaches, as green and unspoiled as any Yorkshire Dale. Once the chimneys of Keighley are left behind, the valley swings northwards. The River Aire, canal and railway all share the same broad valley floor along with the old mill towns – Steeton, Silsden, Croshills, Kildwick, Cononley, Bradley and even Skipton are all situated at some distance from the river itself. These settlements wisely avoided the flood-prone valley in favour of the drier hillsides. The older Airedale mills didn't use

Malham Tarn

Parish church, Kirkby Malham

Churchyard sign, Kirkby Malham

Leeds–Liverpool Canal at Bank Newton

the main river for water power, instead they utilized the fast flowing Pennine streams which run down the nearby hillsides.

However, it was the 127-mile (203 km) Leeds–Liverpool Canal, which, more than anything else, encouraged the growth of the mill towns of Airedale. In 1777, this pioneering canal ran as far as Gargrave, but by 1812 it linked through the Aire Gap to Liverpool. It brought supplies of coal from Lower Airedale mines to fuel the new steam-powered mills. It also enabled large quantities of raw material, including wool and cotton from Liverpool, to be brought in and the finished cloth to be sent out for export.

Skipton, the largest town in the area, was originally a Norman garrison set up to guard the Aire Gap, an important natural crossing point of the Pennines. The town was, and is today, a country market town. But the arrival of the canal in the late 18th century and the railway in the mid 19th century transformed the town into a centre of textile manufacturing. Old mills survive, but many have been converted into warehouses, offices or accommodation and tourism has now taken over

23

View from top of Malham Cove

Airton

24

Limestone paving, Malham

Malham Cove

from heavy industry.

Immediately beyond Skipton, Airedale is once again unspoiled countryside, with only the village of Gargrave representing any significant centre of population. Gargrave is a former coaching town on the old Leeds–Kendal turnpike road and was once an important inland port on the Leeds–Liverpool Canal.

North of Gargrave, Airedale becomes Malhamdale – a narrow, twisting valley of breathtaking countryside. There are many picturesque villages in the area, such as Airton, Kirkby Malham and Malham itself.

Malham is well worth a visit. Here is probably the most spectacular 'Great Scar' limestone scenery to be found in the British Isles, where the Mid Craven Fault has helped to create two famous features – Malham Cove, a great cliff which in effect is the dry bed of a gigantic waterfall (the stream that has been flowing underground emerges here and forms a small pool) and Gordale Scar, which most experts believe to be a collapsed cavern, carved out by a stream. Gordale Scar was one of the leading 'curiosities' of northern England. In the late 18th and early 19th centuries many writers and artists visited the Scar to experience the 'horror' of the immense, juniper-hung ravine. The poet Thomas Gray who came in 1769, confessed that he 'shuddered' at the sight, but also 'thought my trouble richly paid, for the impression will last for life.'

Above this feature lie miles of limestone pavement, in some places, as above Malham Cove, worn smooth by weather and the trampling of thousands of feet, in other places, rough and harsh to the touch. On the high plateau of Malham Moor lies another remarkable phenomenon, Malham Tarn. This is a lake lying on a bed of ancient rock and glacial debris. The rock is far older than the Great Scar limestones of the Cove, but has been lifted above it by the movement of the Earth that produced the Craven Fault (described in the Upper Wharfedale chapter). The Tarn now forms part of a Nature Reserve and Field Study Centre.

This area is also especially rich in archaeological remains – Bronze Age stone circles and field systems going back to Iron Age times, medieval sheep folds, monastic packhorseways and 18th-century enclosures have all left their mark here, telling the story of many ages of human activity and civilization.

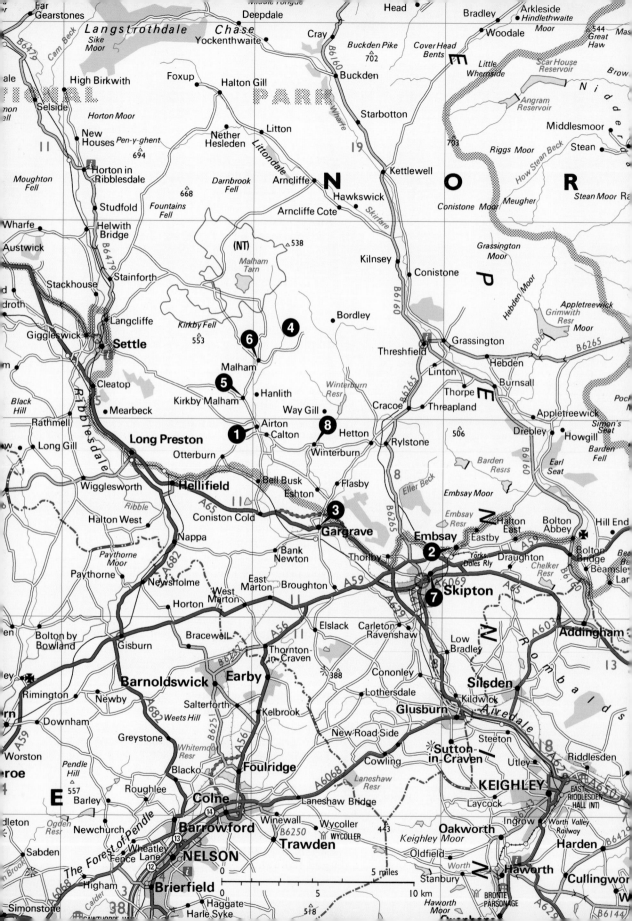

❶ AIRTON

Like Gargrave, Airton has an extensive village green surrounded by old houses and cottages. One of these is a late 17th-century Friends' Meeting House built in 1696 by William and Alice Ellis, linen weavers, which was turned into a Meeting House in 1702. The riverside mill has been converted to residential accommodation. General Lambert, one of Cromwell's greatest generals, was born at nearby Calton in 1615.

❷ EMBSAY STEAM RAILWAY

Some 2 miles (3 km) from Skipton, this linear village with its Elm Tree Square and inn has a popular steam railway. This is the only surviving portion of the former Skipton–Ilkley railway which currently runs for 2 miles (3 km) between Embsay Station and Holywell Halt. Extensions to the line are planned as far as Bolton Abbey. There is a museum of railway memorabilia, a cafeteria and well-stocked bookshop specializing in railway and industrial history. (Museum open all year; Operating days, July, Tues, Sat and Sun; August, Tues–Sun, except Fri; Bank holidays. Phone 0756 794727)

❸ GARGRAVE

Gargrave has a winding main street with tall, old coaching inns, and twin village greens which lead down to the River Aire. The Pennine Way goes through the village centre, and locks on the Leeds–Liverpool Canal form the focal point of a small marina.

❹ GORDALE SCAR

This huge ravine was one of the most popular tourist attractions of nothern England in the 19th century. Well worth visiting for its breath-taking effect.

❺ KIRKBY MALHAM

The village's name suggests that a church was already here in Anglo-Danish times. The present Parish Church that serves the whole of Malhamdale was rebuilt in the 15th century, but there is an 11th-century, dog-tooth-decorated font, a 14th-century muniment chest, a ducking stool and an 'invasion beam' that could be drawn over the south door as a precaution against invading Scots. But the most intriguing feature of all are the carved-stone Celtic Heads on the porch and church wall.

❻ MALHAM

Malham Village has a large car park and National Park centre to cope with the thousands of visitors who arrive by car and coach on almost any day of the year. The village has a good choice of pubs, cafés, outdoor shops, galleries and accommodation, including a youth hostel named after John Dower.

There is a popular walk along the Pennine Way to Malham Cove, where you can enjoy the famous view from the limestone pavement at the summit. Equally popular is the walk along the cul-de-sac lane (difficult for cars) to Gordale Scar. Though a public path exists up the Scar, it is a difficult and dangerous scramble and erosion is now a serious problem.

Longer walks can take in the remarkable Dry Valley to Malham Tarn where there are nature trails through the National Trust woodlands to the Field Centre. There is limited car parking nearby. Footpath maps available at the National Park Centre indicate the huge choice of outstanding walks in the area.

❼ SKIPTON

On every day of the week except for Tuesday and Sundays, Skipton's broad High Street is crammed with a colourful open market. Narrow alleyways lead off the High Street into little precincts of shops, such as Victoria Square, with the Tourist Information Centre, and Craven Court, a shopping arcade. The Craven Museum, in the Victorian Town Hall, has outstanding collections of Dales' lead-mining and wildlife material, archaeological finds from Craven and the medieval town of Skipton. (Open Apr–Sept, Wed–Mon and Sun afternoons only; Oct–Mar, Mon, Wed–Fri, afternoons, Sat. Phone 0756 794079)

Skipton Castle, at the top of the High Street, is one of the best-preserved medieval castles in England, though it was largely rebuilt in the late 17th century by Lady Anne Clifford, the last of the Clifford family, when she repaired the extensive damage done by Cromwell's army. Especially interesting are the twin towers of the Gatehouse within which there is a unique Shell Room packed with shells collected by a Tudor Earl of Cumberland on his Caribbean voyages. The dungeons and the central Conduit Court, where a great yew tree planted by Lady Anne still flourishes, are also intriguing. (Open all year, Mon–Sat and Sun afternoons. Phone 0756 792442)

The canal basin of the Leeds–Liverpool Canal, immediately behind the town centre, is usually packed with pleasure craft. You can follow the towpath along the cul-de-sac Spring Branch, reached from the top of the High Street and leading behind the formidable castle wall. The towpath winds its way between the canal and Eller Beck to Skipton Woods, part of the old castle grounds with pathways and a lake. (Open daily, afternoons only)

There are boat trips along the canal towards Gargrave at most weekends and daily in the summer. ☎ 0756 792809

❽ WINTERBURN

One of the finest late Tudor houses of the Yorkshire Dales is to be found at Friars Head, situated on the Winterburn–Eshton road and built on the site of a Grange of Furness Abbey by the Proctor family, one of whom, Sir Stephen Proctor, went on to build Fountains Hall at Fountains Abbey. (Open all year except some Fridays Oct–Jan. Phone 076586 333

Winterburn Chapel, now a house, was one of the earliest nonconformist chapels in Yorkshire (1694). It is an easy walk along the track from the hamlet to Winterburn Reservoir, whose waters feed into the summit pound of the Leeds-Liverpool Canal near Foulridge by a 9 mile long aqueduct which still functions – a superb piece of early 19th century engineering.

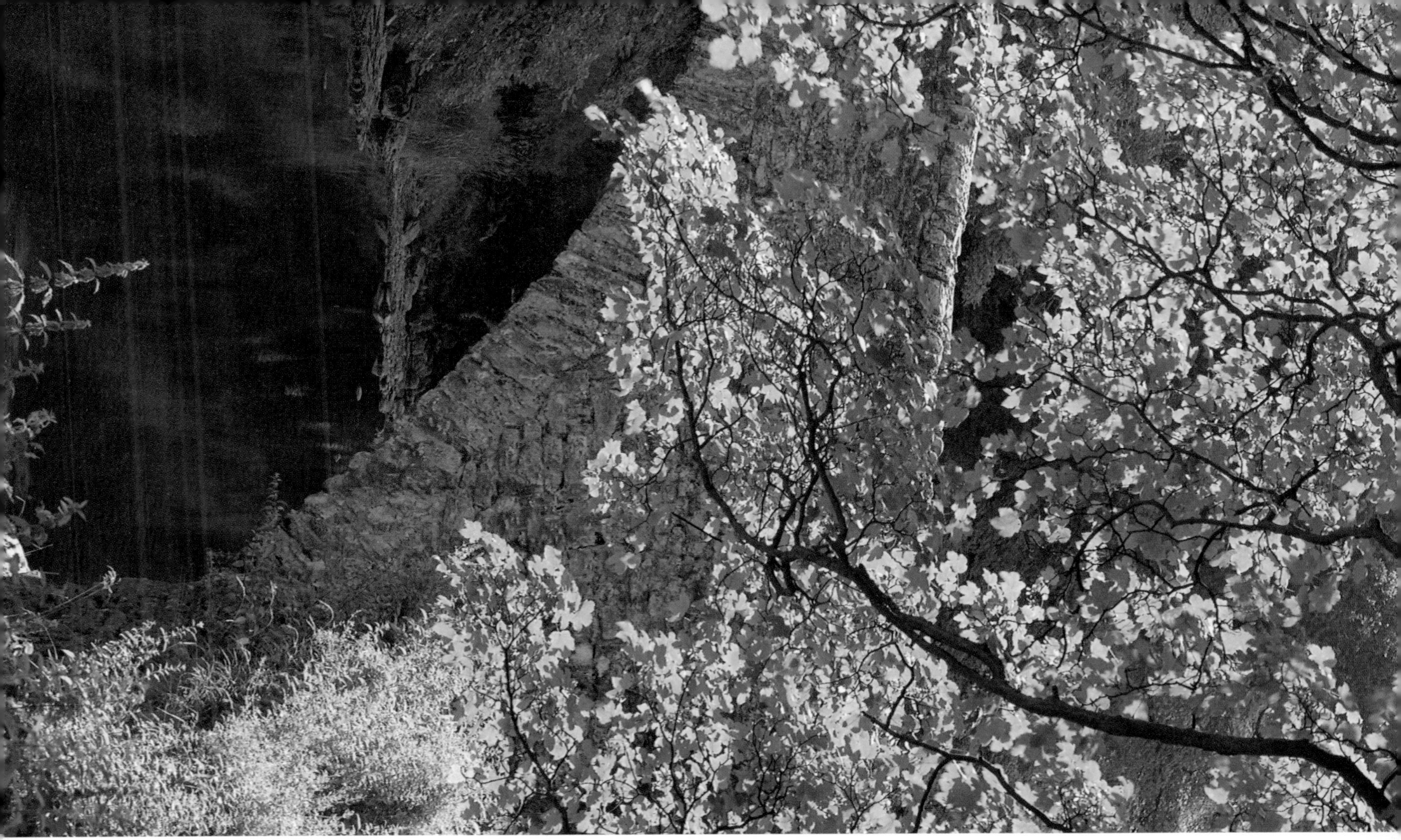

Upper Ribblesdale

Three Ways Through, Ribblesdale

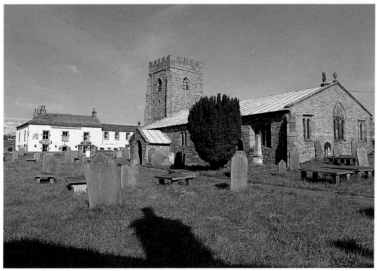

St Oswald's, Horton-in-Ribblesdale

Preceding page: **Packhorse bridge, Stainforth**

Catrigg Force (TC)

The Ribble is, for most of its length, a Lancashire river. It winds its way from the county town of Preston northwards around the Forest of Bowland past Whalley, Clitheroe and Gisburn, before skirting the drumlins – low, round hills formed from glacial waste after the last Ice Age had retreated. The hills now divide Upper Airedale from its neighbouring Ribblesdale. But at Settle the Ribble enters limestone country and as the scenery changes, so too does the character of the river. It becomes a bustling, mountain river, carrying salmon as well as trout.

Settle itself, situated at the Aire Gap, has for many centuries been the 'gateway' of the south-western dales, acting as the centre for passing trade. Its importance grew in 1753, when the Keighley–Kendal Turnpike was completed, bringing coaching traffic to the town. The town is also famous for the Settle–Carlisle railway line. A plaque in the town pays tribute to those men that died during its construction.

A tall, grass-covered crag, Castlebergh, towers over Settle. But Castlebergh, in its turn, is dwarfed by even steeper crags which rise up along Warrendale Knotts and Attermire Scar as a series of spectacular, weathered formations, the views of

View across Langcliffe to Langcliffe Scar (TC)

Stainforth Force and bridge (SW)

which are best enjoyed either by the footpath or the back road to Malham. Reminiscent of a miniature version of the Dolomites, they form an impressive skyline, the peaks looking far more immense than their relatively modest height of around 1300 feet (400 m).

Like so much of the most spectacular scenery of the Yorkshire Dales, including Malhamdale, these crags are part of the exposed line of the Craven Fault and consist of Carboniferous or mountain limestone.

Yet limestone is both Ribblesdale's glory and its greatest problem. Breathtaking, beautiful scenery

there is, but limestone is also prized by industry. As you travel north from Settle it is impossible to ignore the great man-made scars in the limestone. Quarries of gargantuan dimension form huge, unsightly tracts at Giggleswick, Helwith Bridge (where exposures of Silurian slate are also worked as highly prized stone for surfacing roads), Horton-in-Ribblesdale and Ribblehead. The quarries and their heavy traffic are an unfortunate source of visual pollution, but as you travel above and away from them, the dale is as softly beautiful and as green as any of its neighbours.

Spectacular natural features abound. There are

Pen-y-ghent

Alum Pot with Pen-y-ghent in the distance (TC)

Entrance to Alum Pot

View of Settle from Castlebergh Hill

Foredale Quarry (TC)

miles of limestone pavement forming terraces along the higher valley slopes, easily reached by the keen walker prepared to make use of a good choice of higher level footpaths. Watch out for the stunningly rich variety of wild flowers that appear in the spring.

A special feature of Ribblesdale is the remarkable system of caves and potholes which honeycombe the area, coming to the surface in such places as

Thorns Gill

Hunt and Hull Pots near Horton and Alum Pot at Selside. The formation of caves is a complex process. Limestone is a relatively porous rock and the action of rain and frost and particularly the acid flow of rainwater that runs off surface peat soon erodes its way into natural cracks and joints in the rock and eventually forming deep passages which can run for miles underground. They can vary in size from spectacular caverns with a dazzling display of stalactites and stalagmites, to narrow cracks through which only a very slender and agile person can just about squeeze. Many of them are permanently under water, or guarded by terrifying sumps which can only be crossed by intrepid cave divers with breathing equipment.

The top of Ribblesdale, Ribblehead, dominated by its great railway viaduct, is one of the remotest and bleakest landscapes in England. This is a treeless, windswept hillscape in which the bare, sculptured shapes of the fells have a grandeur and remoteness only relieved by secret gills (deep, naturally formed holes in the rock), such as Ling Gill and Thorns Gill, which are as intimate as their surroundings are wild – their rocky sides hang with birch and rowan, and garlanded with prim-roses in spring. Again the word gill reveals the close Nordic ties of this region. Gill is derived from the Old Norse, meaning a steep-sided valley. 33

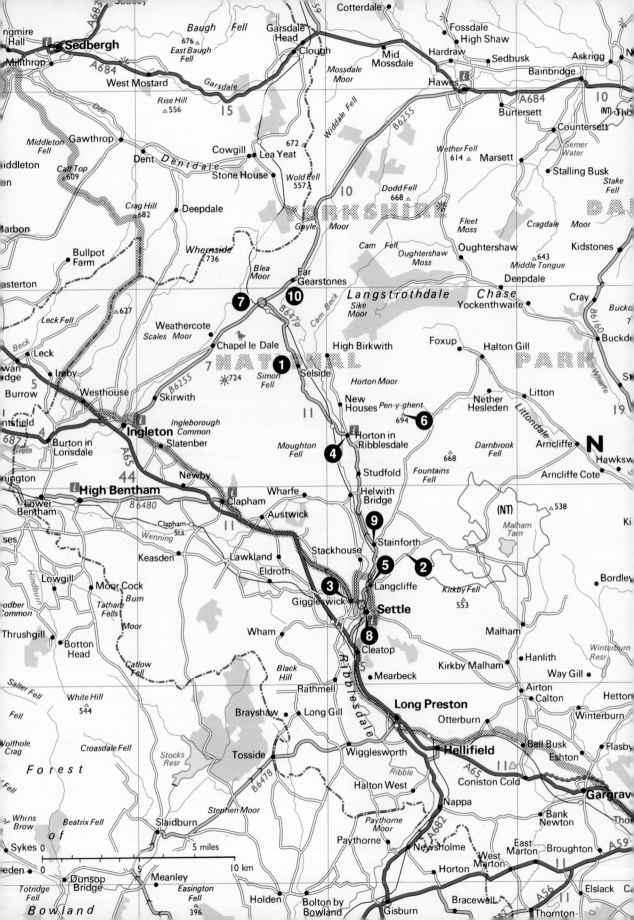

❶ ALUM POT

Upper Ribblesdale is an important area for caving, and even if you don't intend to go underground, it is worth seeing Alum Pot. A 'Pot' or 'pothole' is the Yorkshire name for a limestone chasm. It is easily reached by a footpath from Selside (small admission charge payable at the farm). The chasm is some 190 feet (65 m) deep. Early travellers believed the spray from its waterfall to be the smoke of hellfire itself.

❷ CATRIGG FOSS

Catrigg Foss is one of the most beautiful waterfalls in the Dales. The falls can only be reached by foot along a steep track, Goat Lane, at the top of which a stile leads down a woodland path into a narrow gorge where you'll find the 60-foot (18 m) falls.

❸ GIGGLESWICK

Giggleswick is notable for many fine 17th-century cottages and houses, and also for its 15th-century parish church, dedicated to St Alkelda – a Saxon princess martyred for her faith, whose name is often linked to holy wells. A famous example, the Ebb and Flowing still exists nearby, in a stone trough beside the A65 just below Booker Brow.

❹ HORTON-IN-RIBBLESDALE

Horton-in-Ribblesdale owes its fame to the nearby Three Peaks, including the majestic Pen-y-ghent, over which the Pennine Way winds its way into the village. It is also the starting point of a 24-mile (38 km) challenge walk, the success of which has left severe problems of footpath erosion. The village is a popular centre for walkers, both on the Pennine Way and the Ribble Way, which runs from the coast below Preston to Cam Fell above Ribblehead. ☎ 07296 333

❺ LANGCLIFFE

The attractive village of Langcliffe takes its name from the cliff that lies to the north. It was once a mill village; the former water-powered mills are situated by the river, one of which, Roberts, is still hard at work (though no longer water powered) recycling waste paper for cardboard.

Just north of the village is a unique piece of industrial history – the Hoffman Kiln – a vast, 19th-century, lime kiln which is now being turned into an industrial museum. Although there is no official access to the structure, it can be seen from the footpath which runs alongside it.

❻ PEN-Y-GHENT

The name Pen-y-ghent comes from Welsh meaning 'Hill of the border' – no doubt a reference to the western border of the ancient Celtic kingdom of Brigantia.

The 2273-foot (694 m) high mountain, with its distinctive sphinx-like shape, provides the focus for one of the most popular walks in the north of England. It is best climbed from Horton. Unfortunately, the tramping of walkers' feet is damaging the hillside, so please keep to the waymarked trails and board walks to reduce the risk of further erosion.

❼ RIBBLEHEAD

The most romantic way of reaching Ribblehead is by train on the Settle–Carlisle railway, but only southbound trains call at the station's single surviving platform. This lonely junction of roads from Settle, Ingleton and Hawes is dominated by the vast 24-arch viaduct, behind which rises the highest of the Three Peaks, Whernside.

❽ SETTLE

Settle is one of the most fascinating towns in the Dales, enjoying an impressive setting in the shelter of limestone crags. A colourful market takes place every Tuesday in the square. Settle's most unusual feature is The Shambles, a row of unique double-decker shops and houses, with basement and floor shops, and houses above. They date from the 18th century, but an extra storey was added at the end of the 19th century. There is also a handsome French-style, Victorian town hall (with the Tourist Information Centre), and a remarkable 17th-century town house known as The Folly because of its extravagant blending of architectural styles.

Settle richly repays exploration on foot. There are intriguing courtyards and a network of narrow alleyways, a wealth of Georgian and early 19th-century shops, inns, houses and warehouses. The Museum of North Craven Life in Chapel Street has a range of exhibitions illustrating aspects of local archaeology and history, including some of the major finds at nearby Victoria Cave, which is only a short walk by steep track and footpath from the town centre. (Open Easter–June, Sat and Sun, afternoons only; July–Sept daily, afternoons only. Phone 07292 2854)

A path through an archway from the street behind the Trustee Savings Bank leads to Castlebergh, a narrow, limestone scar. The path zigzags to a superb viewpoint of Settle and Upper Ribblesdale, looking across the valley to the hills of Bowland that form the far horizon.

❾ STAINFORTH

Stainforth is really two villages – Knight Stainforth to the west of the river, now merely a hamlet dominated by a fine 17th-century yeoman's house, and Great Stainforth, the present village linked by the 'stony ford' of the village's name.

The existing packhorse bridge was built in Tudor times to link both communities with an ancient Lancaster–York packhorse way. Great Stainforth, now by-passed by the traffic which once roared through its centre, has a winding main street, old inn and an attractive church.

❿ THORNS GILL

Many people consider Thorns Gill to be the most beautiful packhorse bridge in the Yorkshire Dales. It can only be reached on foot, by a path which leaves the Hawes road, just west of Gearstones farm, about half a mile from Ribblehead, and which runs through a pedestrian gate. The bridge crosses a narrow gill through which the peat-brown beck – the source of the Ribble – rushes.

Lonsdale

Feizor (TC)

Ingleton

Preceding page: **Ruskin's View, Kirkby Lonsdale**

Devil's Bridge, Kirkby Lonsdale

Like Ribblesdale, Lonsdale (home of the River Lune) is also for much of its length a Lancashire dale, with the great city and port of Lancaster at its river's estuary. But in its higher reaches, beyond Kirkby Lonsdale and past Casterton, Barbon and Middleton, this most gentle of rivers enters true Dales country. Although never quite entering Yorkshire, the river, around Sedbergh, forms a boundary with what used to be the old West Riding when Westmorland was still in existence. It still forms the natural, if not political boundary of the Dales region – the point where the character of the countryside changes to Morecambe Bay and Lakeland, and away from the limestone hills to the east.

Ribblesdale runs through countryside which is undulating rather than truly hilly, and although the well-wooded dale exudes a sense of civilisation, the peak of Ingleborough dominates the countryside, acting as a constant reminder that a wilder countryside exists beyond the deceptively gentle valley.

Feizor and Pott Scar (TC)

Kirkby Lonsdale

Ingleborough

Barbondale

It was the view of Lonsdale from Kirkby Lonsdale churchyard, with the mountains in the background, which led John Ruskin, in 1875, to remark in his somewhat over-effusive way that it was 'one of the loveliest scenes in England – therefore in the world. Whatever moorland hill, and sweet river, and English forest foliage can be at their best is gathered here. . .' Understandably, the view promptly became a favourite spot for visitors wanting to see this 'loveliest scene' for themselves, and since then the local tourist interests

Thornton Force

have ensured that 'Ruskin's View' has been clearly signposted from Kirkby Lonsdale town centre. What they don't tell you is that Ruskin followed up this idyll with angry protests about fences and benches that had been provided. But the view remains, and the largely Georgian market town, with its ancient river bridge, is where you can best enjoy the scenery.

The River Lune has a number of significant tributaries that are very much Dales – and even Yorkshire rivers. The first of these is the Wenning, which twists its way past Hornby and Wennington and as far east as Austwick and Clapham where the village becks tumble into the infant river.

If Kirkby Lonsdale is linked with Ruskin, Clapdale and the village of Clapham is associated with the Farrer family – a remarkable family of landowners, philanthropists and scientists, the most celebrated of which was Reginald Farrer (1880–1940). Many gardeners will recognize him as the world famous plant collector and botanist, who has several plant species named after him and who did much to help popularize rock gardening in Britain. It was his ancestors who dammed the lake that now forms the centrepiece of the Ingleborough Estate. His successor still manages much of the magnificent area of open common land that forms the southern slopes of Ingle-

Clapham (SW)

View of Feizor Woods and Warrendale Knotts (TC)

Robin Proctor's Scar, near Austwick (TC)

borough mountain.

The landscape of this area is pockmarked with caves and potholes, with miles of superb limestone pavement rising all the way to the summit of Ingleborough itself.

Austwick Beck an insignificant stream, flows through the huge, limestone gorge of Crummockdale. This area is a paradise for both hillwalker and botanist, and indeed geologists. For immediately above Austwick, at Norber, there are the great, lichen-covered Norber Erratics – gigantic Silurian slate boulders from Crummockdale which were carried above the newer limestone pavement by glacial ice and abandoned as the ice retreated,

to remain like gigantic, natural sculptures on the plateau.

Another important tributary of the Lune is the Greta which, once east of Burton in Lonsdale and Ingleton, splits into the smaller Greta and the Doe to provide perhaps the most spectacular series of waterfalls in the British Isles, the Ingleton Waterfalls, which became popular with Victorian visitors.

Again the area will be of interest to geologists as the fast flowing streams have eroded not only through the underlying limestone, but through deeper Silurian and Ordovician slates into complex Cambrian and pre-Cambrian strata.

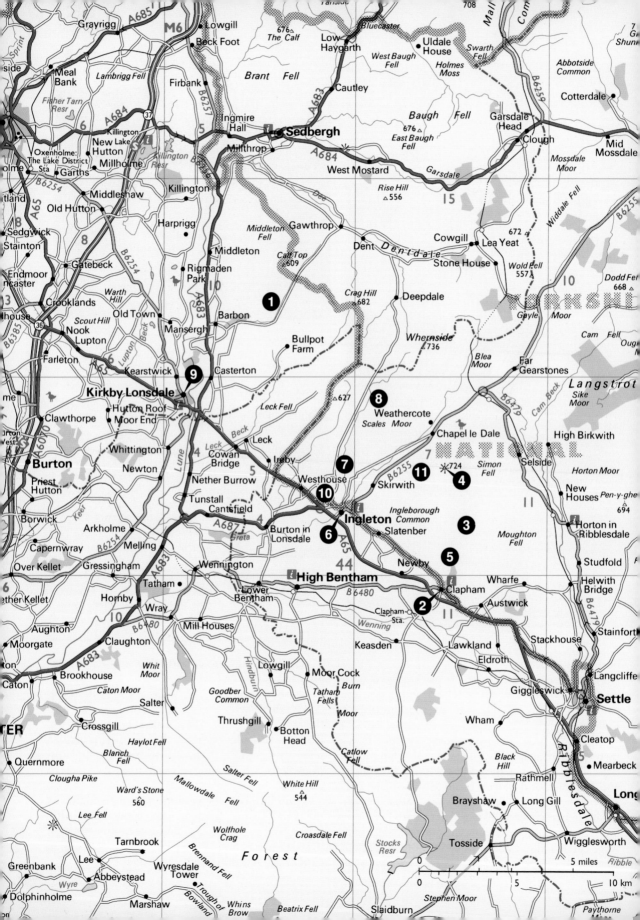

❶ BARBONDALE

The River Barbon, a tributary of the Lune, follows a major geological feature, the Great Pennine Fault. The fault gives Barbondale a very distinctive character, with a steeply-graded slope on the left side of the narrow valley compared to the gentler, more rounded hillside to the right. Barbon village is a compact community, with a pleasant pub and Victorian church.

❷ CLAPHAM

A shrub-lined stream crossed by hump-backed bridges makes a natural focal point of this delightful village. The main street of mainly 18th-century houses and cottages lies along each side of the beck. At the top of the village there is a Regency church and a series of waterfalls which still provide hydro-electric power.

❸ GAPING GILL

Gaping Gill is the largest cavern in Britain, with a central chamber some 450 feet (140 m) long and 95 feet (29 m) high and wide. It also has Britain's highest waterfall – albeit underground. The waterfall links with no less than about 9 miles (15 km) of underground passages. Although it is easy to reach the mouth of Gaping Gill by footpath from Clapham (the narrow entrance is extremely dangerous – keep well away), only experienced cavers can descend into the cave, except on spring and summer bank holiday weekends when local caving clubs arrange a winch and gantry and bosun's chair, and well-protected visitors are winched down to the bottom of the cave.

❹ INGLEBOROUGH

For many years, it was assumed that Ingleborough was England's highest mountain, so impressively does this 2373-foot (723 m) high peak with its gritstone cap rise from the Wenning valley. The mountain was the site of an Iron-Age hill village, probably built for defence against the Romans. The remains of its defensive wall and hut circles can still be seen. The name 'Ingle' denotes fire and for centuries the mountain was used as a beacon to warn of danger.

❺ INGLEBOROUGH ESTATE AND CAVE

A short walk from Clapham village leads to the Ingleborough Estate, for which a small entrance charge is made. (Open mid Feb–mid Jan daily. Phone 04685 242) Ingleborough Hall, the former seat of the Farrers of Clapham, is now an outdoor educational centre. Two fine columns in the entrance hall are made of fossilized, black Dent marble, quarried locally. The village is a popular starting point for walks to Ingleborough Cave, Gaping Gill and Ingleborough Mountain. The lakeside walk along the old carriage drive passes ornamental woodlands, shrubs and a small grotto. There are also superb displays of rhododendrons, planted by Reginald Farrer himself.

Ingleborough Cave lies at the top of the estate. This was opened in 1837 when Mr Farrer ordered a wall of stalagmite to be broken down. This revealed a magnificent cave, containing a series of chambers. The features have such evocative names as Pillar Hall, the Gothic arch, the Long Gallery and the Pool of Reflections. (Open Apr–Oct daily; winter weekends only)

❻ INGLETON

This old market village, with its narrow main street and scattered cottages, was once important in the days when its Annual Fair was famous for its leather goods and oatmeal. A metal hook, used for fastening the bull during the barbaric pastime of bull baiting, is still to be seen in the village square.

❼ INGLETON WATERFALLS

In 1885 a group of local people got together in Ingleton with the express purpose of developing the village for tourists. They formed themselves into the Ingleton Improvement Company, opening up a series of carefully built walkways through the twin gorges of the Rivers Greta and Doe, exposing spectacular waterfalls and cataracts.

At Thornton Force it is possible to stand behind the waterfall. A small entrance fee is payable. Many of the waterfalls can only be reached on foot. Take care at all times as the paths can be slippery, particlularly in wet weather.

❽ KINGSDALE

The valley of the River Doe above Ingleton becomes Kingsdale, a little known valley of great beauty. There are fine walks up onto Braida Garth or on moorland tracks towards Ireby and the Leck valley. Yordas Cave, which was once a major tourist attraction and painted by Turner, is now closed for safety reasons.

❾ KIRKBY LONSDALE

Kirkby Lonsdale is notable for its fine Georgian and early Victorian buildings. It has a 13th-century parish church, an attractive market square (market day is Thursday) and a wide range of shops and cafés. A Victorian Fair is held in the town each year during the first weekend of September.

The ancient bridge across the Lune, no longer used for motor traffic, dates at least from the 14th century. According to legend it was built by the Devil for an old woman to allow her cattle to cross providing she gave him the soul of the first creature to cross. But the old woman outwitted the Devil by tossing a bun across that was retrieved by her little dog and the Devil left in a fury. ⧉ (in Main Street) 05242 71437

❿ THORNTON IN LONSDALE

Almost Ingleton's twin village, Thornton lies immediately on the other side of the Greta. The village has a fine 15th-century church and an equally impressive pub, the Marton Arms, that dates from 1679.

⓫ WHITE SCAR CAVES

White Scar Cave was discovered in 1923, and its narrow passageways were enlarged to create a show cave. There are impressive stalactites and stalagmites, scoured pools and flow stones. One stalagmite has been dated at 225,000 years old. The Caves have recently been extended. (Open Mar–Nov daily. Phone 05242 41244)

Dentdale and Garsdale

Interior of Quaker Meeting House at Brigflatts

Sedgwick Memorial, Dent

Quaker Meeting House, Brigflatts

Dent Head Viaduct

Preceding page: Howgill Fells and Long Rigg Beck

Cottages in Dent

Dentdale is the only major Yorkshire Dale that runs north-westwards. The River Dee winds its way from the shoulders of Whernside – the third of the Three Peaks – and Wold Fell to meet the Rawthey and the Lune west of Sedbergh.

This is one of the most intimately beautiful of the Yorkshire Dales, albeit now claimed within Cumbria. Its main road is little more than a narrow lane which meanders first of all alongside the river and then later between tall hedgerows that in spring shelter primroses and dog violets. The back lane between Cowgill and Dent is only just wide enough for a car.

Perhaps because it collects the mild rains of the west, this is one of the greenest of the Dales. It also differs in character for another reason, having been originally settled by Vikings (rather than Anglian farmers) in the 9th century. The Vikings'

Quaker graveyard, Brigflatts

long narrow strip farms, each with a section of fell, a farmhouse on the spring line and fertile, bottom riverside land are still to be seen in outline.

Many of the farmhouses date back to their last rebuilding in the 17th century, and footpath links between them, part of which is the Dales Way, offer a delightful way of discovering the dale.

One curious feature of the valley is the fact that the River Dee, for much of its length flows underground for all but the rainiest periods, using subterranean chasms and passages, only to emerge from springs and sink holes, leaving a rocky limestone bed and deep pools.

Sedbergh

Fell ponies on Jeffrey Mount, Shap Fell (TC)

Fox's Pulpit, Firbank Fell (SW)

The Howgill Fells above Sedbergh

Much of this limestone is an unusual bluey-black in colour because of its carbon content, and in the last century was quarried locally, being much prized for items such as fireplaces and ornamental shelves. When highly polished it reveals delicate patterns of fossils.

Dentdale only has one village, Dent – more correctly described as Dent Town. It was here in 1785 that one of the greatest figures of Victorian geological science, Professor Adam Sedgwick, was born. He was the son of the local vicar. Educated at the village Grammar school and at Sedbergh, he eventually became Woodwardian Professor of Geology at Cambridge University, a post he held for 55 years until his death in 1873. In addition to

becoming world famous for major geological discoveries, he was a great teacher, educational reformer, a close friend of Queen Victoria and Prince Albert, and a remarkable local historian and benefactor of his native dale.

It was Sedgwick who first described the complex geology of the Lake District, and first revealed the fault system running along Barbondale and through Dentdale that divides the Carboniferous sandstones and limestone of the Dales from the harder, older Silurian slates of the Lake District.

Sedbergh, which lies in a great bowl of the hills formed where the rivers Dee, Rawthey, Clough and Lune meet, is the most important town in the north-western dales, and the natural centre for

Norber Scar, erratic boulder

Baugh Fell

Drinking fountain, Sedbergh

exploring the Howgills. This area was a hotbed of the Quaker movement in the latter half of the 17th century after the prophet and visionary George Fox preached outside the parish church in Sedbergh and later on Firbank Fell above the town. Shortly before that, he claimed to have had a vision (on Pendle Hill in nearby Ribblesdale) and excited crowds flocked to hear him speak wherever he went.

The great, green grassy dome-like hills behind Sedbergh are the Howgill Fells, ancient commons on old, much-weathered Silurian slates and flags, which rise to over 2000 feet (610 m) to such summits as Winder, The Calf and Brant Fell. All the hillsides are largely unfenced, crossed by paths and sheep tracks and provide magnificent mountain walking along high, open ridges away from the crowds.

Two valleys run at each side of the Howgills, the Upper Lune Gorge and the Rawthey. The riverside path, quiet lanes and old Roman road of the Upper Lune suddenly, beyond Crook of Lune Bridge, give way to the incessant roar of the M6 motorway and the West Coat main line electric railway racing over Shap to Scotland.

The Rawthey Valley suffers no such disturbance, its winding, mountain road to Kirkby Stephen (A683) has some spectacular views, particularly when there is a light fall of snow on the fell tops.

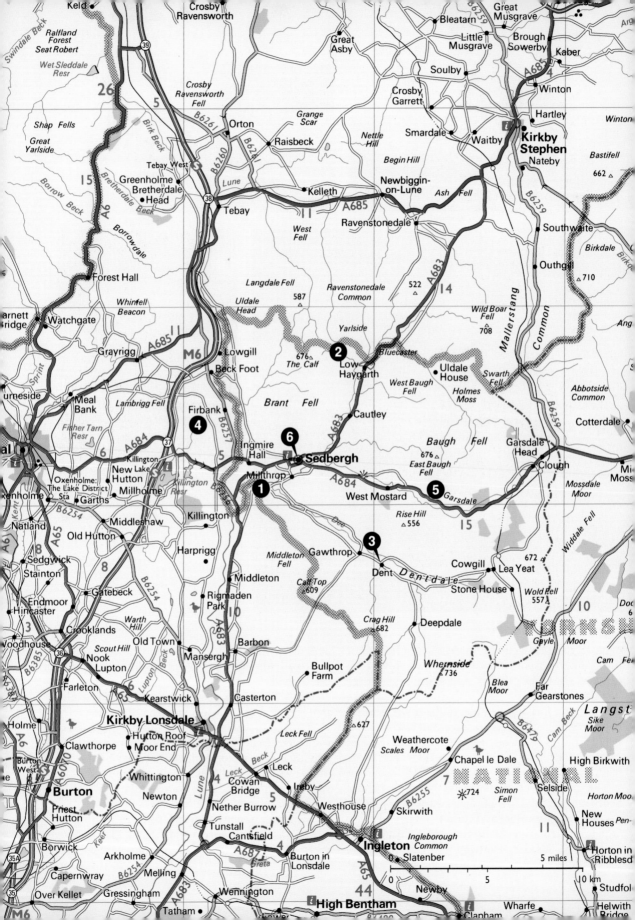

❶ BRIGFLATTS

At Brigflatts, about 2 miles (3 km) west of Sedbergh off the A683, you'll find one of the oldest Quaker Meeting Houses in England. Dating from 1675, when it was first built, the Friends were too poor to build a ceiling, and so they lined the roof with common moss, only adding the gallery in 1711. As the Act of 1670 made non-conformist meetings illegal, Friends came from several miles to worship in this remote place, risking arrest for their belief.

Visitors are always welcome at the Meeting House and its quiet garden, and regular services are held. It is best reached on foot by riverside and fieldpath from Sedbergh; a leaflet at the National Park Centre in Sedbergh gives details.

❷ CAUTLEY SPOUT

Cautley Spout is one of the highest and most spectacular waterfalls in the Yorkshire Dales. It is best reached from the Cross Keys Temperance Hotel on the A683 Kirkby road from Sedbergh, crossing a field path to the narrow waterfall which plunges nearly a 1000 feet (304 m) in stages alongside the great rocky wall of Cautley Crag. The climb by the waterfall is severe, and can be dangerous in wet weather.

❸ DENT TOWN

Many people regard the little township of Dent as being the most beautiful in the Yorkshire Dales. It has a cobbled main street, with colourwashed cottages, although the picturesque balconies where the famous 'terrible knitters' produced their hand-knitted stockings and hats by the score have long since gone. A boulder-fountain of pink Shap granite in the main street stands as a memorial to the Dales' greatest son, Professor Adam Sedgwick. Although he is actually buried in Norwich, there is a memorial plaque to him on the wall of the parish church in Dent Town. The church itself, although much restored, dates from medieval times.

The town has a choice of cafés and two excellent inns. There is a well-equipped specialist outdoor shop at Rise Mill, and you can also visit Dent Glass, to see a variety of glassware being made. About a mile along the Sedbergh road are the Dent Craft Workshops where traditional dales pottery and textiles are made. (Open daily. Jan–Feb, open Sat and Sun only. Phone 05875 400)

❹ FOX'S PULPIT

In 1652, following his great vision on the summit of Pendle Hill in Lancashire, George Fox travelled through the North of England preaching a new vision of Christianity. When he eventually reached Sedbergh, he led his followers to the summit of nearby Firbank Fell where he preached a passionate sermon. He later declared that 'the greatest part of a thousand people were convinced that day'.

This gathering was the starting point of what later became known as the Society of Friends or more colloquially The Quakers. This has become, over the years a worldwide movement that is still enormously influential today.

The simple rock on which Fox preached in 1652, known as Fox's Pulpit, can still be seen. Take the narrow lane over Firbank Fell (off the A684) about 2 miles (3 km) along the road on the right hand side. It is a walk of a few yards through a marked fieldgate.

❺ GARSDALE

Garsdale, to the east of Sedbergh, is a long, scattered community without any focal point. The road through Garsdale gradually rises to Garsdale Head where, close by the isolated station on the Settle–Carlisle line and the lonely Moorcock Inn, Garsdale blends into Upper Wensleydale. To the north lies the vast, empty expanse of Baugh Fell and the secluded valley of Grisedale, 'the dale that died', where no more than a couple of solitary farms survive.

Two places of special interest between Sedbergh and Garsdale are Pennine Tweeds and the Sedgwick Trail. Pennine Tweeds is a traditional woollen mill producing quality tweeds and a variety of garments for sale. (Open summer daily; winter, Mon–Sat. Phone 0539 620558)

The Sedgwick Trail starts at the lay-by by the cattle grid at Garsdale Foot, just 3 miles (5 km) from Sedbergh on the A683 road. It explores some of the complex geological phenomena in the area, first observed by Professor Sedgwick in the 1830s.

❻ SEDBERGH TOWN

Sedbergh has its own special connection with the Lakeland poets – it was here that John Wordsworth, William's son, was sent to school, and where Hartley Coleridge, Samuel Taylor Coleridge's son, and a poet in his own right, worked as a schoolmaster before being sacked for drunkeness.

Sedbergh School continues to flourish as one of the most famous public schools in the North of England, and its original handsome neo-classical school building, now the Library, stands on the Dent road. Since the time of Adam Sedgwick and Hartley Coleridge the buildings and extensive playing fields have expanded to cover much of the town to give Sedbergh a college town atmosphere.

Just behind the narrow, cobbled main street and shops are narrow courtways concealing yards that date from Tudor times, including an unaltered, Elizabethan chimney and a surviving weavers' gallery. The parish church is as ancient as it looks, going back to Norman times, but with many 14th-century additions.

Like Dent, Sedbergh offers superb opportunities for the walker. There are terrific walks across the magnificent, wild expanse of the Howgill Fells, and also along the riverside by the Rawthey and Dee, and farther ahead to the Lune where the Dales Way twists its way towards the Lake District. A particularly lovely area lies to the north of Killington Bridge, on the B6256 about 3 miles (5 km) west of the town. Now a public access area, the path goes past deep pools of the River Lune. This is an area where the hidden valley is a source of great peace and beauty. ☎ (Sedbergh) 05396 20125

Swaledale

Preceding page: Gunnerside

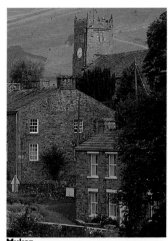

Muker

Barn near Gunnerside

Richmond

Langthwaite, Arkengarthdale (SW)

View of Richmond from Holly Hill

When J. M. W. Turner, arguably England's greatest painter, undertook a sketching tour of the North of England in 1816, he approached the town of Richmond, in Swaledale, over the brow of the hill to the south of the town along what is now the Hudswell road. The view Turner captured of the little grey town on the hill with its castle and tall 12th-century keep, high above the wooded gorge of the Swale, was later transformed into one of his most magical paintings. But the soft greens and sombre greys of Swaledale have been transformed into the brilliant light and the golds of Italy, perspectives altered, cliffs heightened.

Turner was responding, in his highly idiosyncratic and imaginative way, to the inherent drama of Swaledale's landscape. Above Richmond Bridge, the Swale flows through a densely wooded valley, much of it now protected woodland, until, past Grinton, the dale opens out and splits. The Arkle Beck runs north-westwards to form Arkengarthdale, while the main valley of the Swale forms a serpentine course westwards past such villages as Healaugh, Low Row, Gunnerside and Muker to Keld at the head of the dale.

Despite its picturesque appearance, the River Swale is in fact one of the most ferocious rivers in all England. It is fed by moorland streams and becks that rise with alarming speed. They have a tendency to flash flooding and bursting their banks after heavy rain or melting snows, often tearing away walls and embankments and destroying bridges.

The power of the streams was used in the earlier days of lead mining, an industry which was particularly strong in Swaledale. A moorland beck would be dammed, and the water suddenly released to allow its scouring power to uncover mineral bearing rock or galena which lies in vertical seams along the hillsides. The process was called 'hushing' and great scars or 'hushes' are still visible in the Swaledale landscape, together with more extensive remains of later, deep mining activity such as great spoil tips, remains of washing floors, crushing mills, powder houses, storage bays, smelt mills and at Grinton a massive peat house where peat was stored and dried for use in the smelt mill.

Lead mining was at its peak in Swaledale between the 16th and the late 19th centuries, when dwindling supplies of ore and cheap Spanish imports forced closure of the mines and

River Swale at Grinton

Grinton church

Marrick Priory

Easby Abbey

severe economic hardship among the mining communities of Swaledale. This resulted in the migration of around two-thirds of the population, to the growing cities of Durham and Lancashire and, in many cases, to the United States and Canada.

The scattered villages and chapels remain in their dramatically beautiful settings and now attract tourists by the thousands. But what has also remained has been the other mainstay of the traditional dales economy – hill farming. An outstanding feature of Upper Swaledale is the traditional patterns that are made across the valley floors and hillsides by small herb and flower-rich meadows, each enclosed by drystone walls and with a small stone barn where the hay was stored and cattle wintered. Modern farming methods now practised mean that many of these barns are disused, and could easily become ruins or be demolished. However, the National Park Authority and Ministry of Agriculture now co-operate to assist Dales farmers, with the help of building conservation grants, to preserve what is a unique landscape feature.

Fittingly, the present motif used by the Yorkshire Dales National Park for its logo is the head

A cottage in Grinton

18th-century window, Reeth

Keld

Angram

of the black-faced Swaledale 'tup' or ram. This is a particularly hardy breed of sheep with a thick, wiry fleece, which may have originated in breeds which go back more than a 1000 years to Viking times. The Swaledale has the constitution to withstand the rigours of a long and harsh Dales winter on the high fells. The breed is carefully protected by local farmers and stockbreeders, and animals are judged at the annual Muker Show each September, thus keeping alive a vital source of British hill sheep stock and a tradition of Dales husbandry, reflected in a unique landscape heritage.

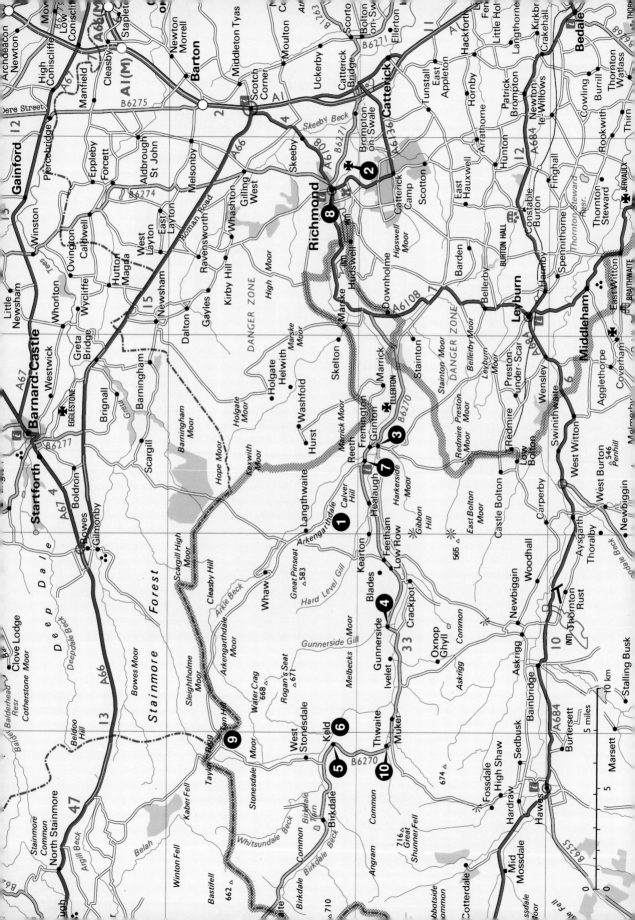

❶ ARKENGARTHDALE

Arkil, son of Gospatrick owned land here before the Norman Conquest and gave his name to this remote Yorkshire dale. The road out of Arkengarthdale down to Healaugh may be familiar to those who watch the James Herriot series – it features in the opening sequence.

Langthwaite, with its little inn, is the only community in the dale large enough to be called a village. Others such as Arkle Town, Whaw, and the evocatively named Booze, are no more than remnants of former lead-mining settlements.

❷ EASBY ABBEY

Easby Abbey, about a mile below Richmond, was founded in 1155 by Roald, Constable of Richmond Castle. It survived until dissolution by Henry VIII's officers in 1535. The extensive ruins have much Norman work, beautifully decorated east window tracery, the remains of cloisters and infirmary buildings. The parish church which dates from the late 12th century is located in the monastic gardens. The Abbey's most notable feature is a replica of the Easby Cross, an Anglo-Saxon cross from around 800 AD, the original of which is in the Victoria and Albert Museum. (Open Apr–Sept daily; Oct–Mar, Tues–Sun)

❸ GRINTON CHURCH

Known as the 'Mother Church' of Swaledale, this ancient church once served the whole of Swaledale. The building dates from Norman times, though it probably stands on a pre-Christian site. Some of its interesting features include a Jacobean-style pulpit and some fine stained glass, both medieval and Victorian.

Most remarkable of all is the ancient Corpse Way which used to lead from Keld at the head of the dale to Grinton. Because this was the only consecrated ground in medieval times, the dead were carried here from remote farms and hamlets in wicker baskets along ancient tracks, with stone slabs at intervals on which the body could be rested as the journey often took two days.

❹ GUNNERSIDE

Gunnerside, named after the 10th-century Anglo-Viking chieftain, Gunnar, is the largest village in the dale. Many of the farmhouses, for example at Winter Ings, are fascinating examples of the dual economy of much of Swaledale during the 17th and 18th centuries. The farmers would work in the local mines in the winter months and look after their farms during the summer. It's worth visiting the Swaledale Woollens shop at nearby Muker where farm-knitted gloves, scarves, sweaters and hats are produced. (Open all year daily. Phone 0748 86251)

❺ KELD

The name 'Keld' is Old Norse for well or spring. This little dalehead community on the Pennine Way focuses around a tiny square. It is a magnificent centre for walks, either down to the nearby waterfalls of Kisdon, Catrake and Wainwath, or over into Birkdale or Stonesdale.

❻ KISDON FORCE

Kisdon Hill forms an unusual geological feature. The original valley of the River Swale to the south was blocked by glacial ice and the river forced its way around the northern side, creating an isolated hill. The erosive actions of the river carving its way into the softer limestone has created a series of waterfalls, of which Kisdon Force is the most famous.

❼ REETH

Standing close to the confluence of the Swale and Arkel Beck, Reeth with its extensive village green, serves both Upper Swaledale and Arkengarthdale as a centre. A former market town, Reeth's three-storey shops and inns along High Row bear witness to its former prosperity at the height of the lead-mining boom. Reeth is the home of the Swaledale Folk Museum which has outstanding collections of material illustrating aspects of Swaledale history, most especially hill-farming, lead mining and Methodism in the dale. (Open Good Fri–Oct daily. Phone 0748 84373) 🖪 Phone 0748 84517

❽ RICHMOND

When Alan the Red, the Breton warlord, built his castle here in 1071, he laid the foundation of a Norman garrison town, the strategic importance of which continued through the centuries. The town is a historian's and architect's delight, with medieval streets, courts and 'wynds', old churches including the remains of a Friary, fashionable 18th-century terraces, mock-Gothic follies and a bustling market place. The Georgian Theatre is the finest preserved theatre of its period in England. It seats 200 and holds the largest and oldest set of painted scenery in Britain. (Museum open May–Sept, Mon–Fri, Sat and Bank Hols, mornings only; Sun, afternoons only. Phone 0748 3021) Also worth visiting is the Richmondshire Museum in Ryders' Wind. This details the history of the area since 1071, as well as having the set of the surgery used in the BBC series *All Creatures Great and Small*. (Open Easter–Oct daily, Bank Hols and school hols, Mon–Fri, mornings only ♿) The Green Howards' Museum in Trinity Church Square houses military equipment dating from 1688. (Open Feb, Mon–Fri; Mar and Nov, Mon–Sat; Apr–Oct, Mon–Sat and Sun afternoons. Phone 0748 2133 ♿). Any trip to Richmond must include a visit to the castle itself. Much of the original Norman stonework has survived due to the castle's relatively peaceful history. (Open Apr–Sept daily; Oct–Mar, Tues–Sun. Phone 0748 2493 ♿)

❾ TAN HILL INN

Tan Hill is the site of England's highest inn at 1732 feet (528 m) above sea level. This remote inn at a lonely crossroads at the head of Stonesdale has its own coal pits and is often cut off by winter snows for weeks at a time.

❿ THWAITE

The hamlet of Thwaite lies at the bottom of the Buttertubs Pass, a spectacular mountain road from Hawes in Wensleydale which takes its name from a series of limestone formations by the roadside which are likened to buttertubs.

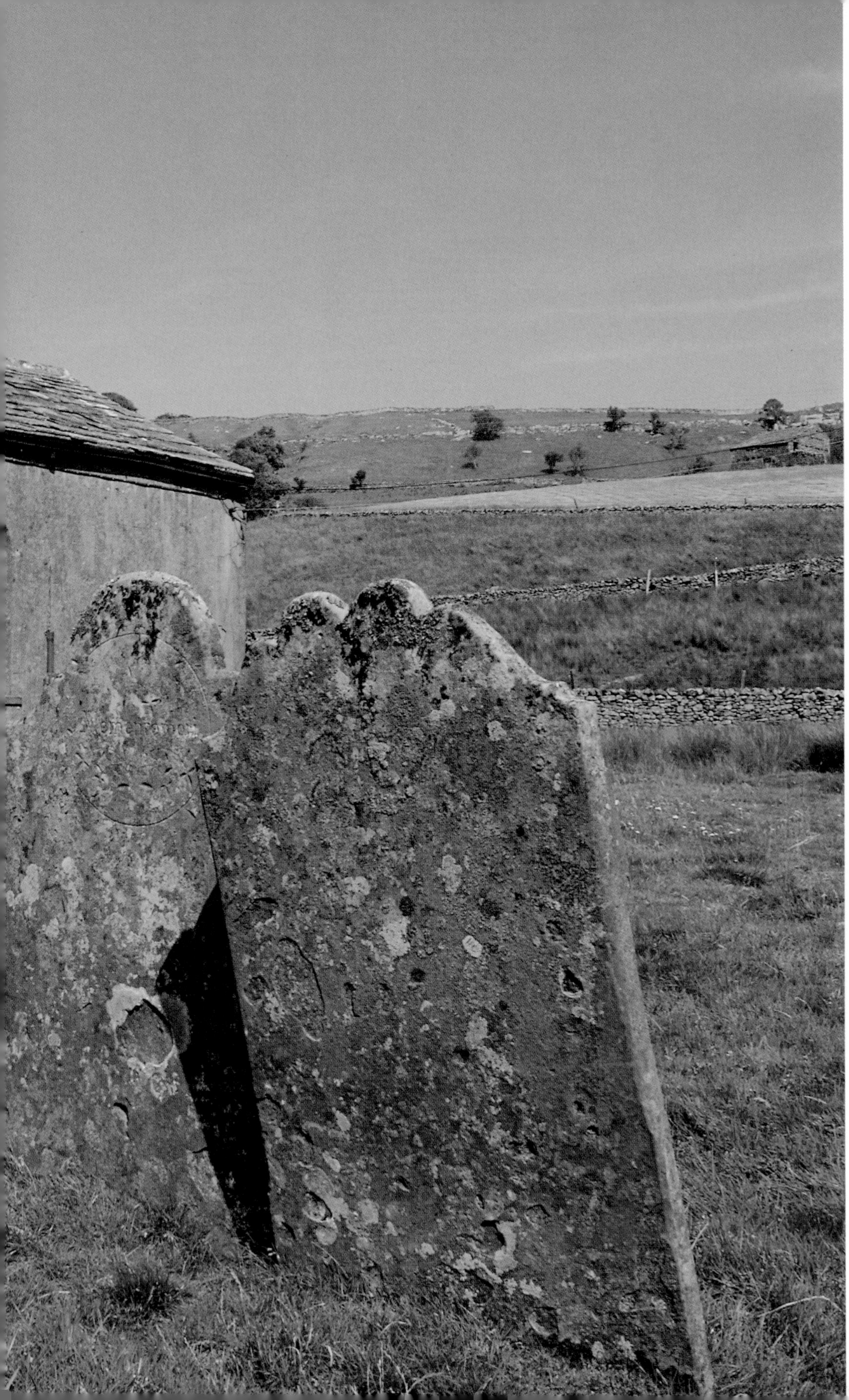

Wensleydale

Farmland, near Bainbridge

Askrigg (BS)

Preceding page: Lund's Church

Country fair, Wensleydale

Aysgarth Falls (BS)

The original name for this sizeable dale was Yoredale, after the River Ure or Yore. The name Wensleydale, though ancient in origin, was the name of a relatively modest mid-dale village which subsequently gave its name not only to the dale, but also to the well-known cheese and a hardy breed of long-fleeced sheep that are becoming increasingly popular among farmers due to their ability to withstand even the harshest winter conditions.

One of the largest, broadest and most signifi-cant of all the Yorkshire Dales, Wensleydale begins at Ure Head Springs. This is a series of brackish pools and peat bogs close to Aisgill on the Cumbria-Yorkshire border high on the side of Abbotside Fell. The tiny river Ure destined eastwards for the Humber and the North Sea, meanders south, parallel to the Settle–Carlisle railway and the Garsdale–Kirkby Stephen road, before turning dramatically eastwards towards the North Sea below Cotter End.

The hills along each side of a surprisingly

Gayle (SW)

St Andrew's churchyard, Aysgarth

broad valley, have that characteristic flat-topped appearance, with a jutting cap or lip of hard gritstone. Underneath these hills are what appear to be gigantic steps that finally yield to a great sloping fellside down to the valley floor. These were features that were described so accurately by the great Yorkshire geologist John Phillips when he wrote of the Yoredale series of rocks that they were 'alternating layers of weather-resistant gritstone or hard sandstones, alternating between softer limestones that have eroded to give the hills that special shape, different in appearance to the crags and scars formed by the huge beds of exposed Mountain Limestone of the southern dales.'

Phillips covered most of Swaledale and Wensleydale on foot in order to describe the geology of the region in his great work *Geology of Yorkshire*, and a rambler or walker who climbs out of the valleys and onto the fells still has the best view of all of this most typical of Yorkshire Dales, with summits such as Wether Fell,

Hawes

Shop sign and walking sticks, Leyburn

Cottage doorway, Bellerby

Fortified farmhouse near Leyburn

Bolton Castle

Semerwater (SW)

Yorburgh, Addleburgh, and Pen Hill making an impressive line along the southern flank of the valley.

Wensleydale has several major tributary valleys, all of which are fully fledged dales in their own right. They include Widdale, Cotterdale, with its fine waterfalls, Fossdale, Sleddale, Bishopdale, Apedale, Coverdale and Colsterdale — dales country, indeed.

Like Swaledale, much of Upper Wensleydale has kept its patterns of drystone walls (built in this valley with a special pattern of their own) and scattered barns.

Sheep are important, with Wensleydale sheep, a relatively new cross-breed, gaining in popularity particularly for knitting and hand weaving. The more fertile pastures of the dale are, not surprisingly, fine dairy country, and the coming of the railway to Wensleydale in the 1860s led to the increase of milk production in order to supply London by overnight express train (Express Dairies and Eden Vale are two household names that originated in the Dales region) and in the manufacture of the characteristic fine creamy white cheese. Originally, Wensleydale was a farmhouse cheese which according to legend was introduced by the monks of Jervaulx Abbey as a cheese made from goats' milk.

Cheesemaking lore has it that the true, tangy flavour of Wensleydale cheese can only be achieved if the cows whose milk is used for the cheese have grazed on pastures with a limestone soil. Grazing conditions in Wensleydale are, of course, perfect. It was only from about the turn of the century that the cheese was actually produced for markets outside the dale. The first Wensleydale cheese factory was located in a converted Hawes textile mill by Gayle Beck.

The story of Wensleydale cheese will forever be linked to that of Kit Calvert of Hawes. He organized a delegation of Dales farmers who travelled to London in the 1940s to meet the Minister of Agriculture in a successful lobby to preserve the distinctive style of Wensleydale cheese making. He later rescued the factory from bankruptcy and pioneered the marketing of single, round one-pound cheeses now so popular. Kit was a great book collector (his shop survives in Hawes' main street) and an authority on Dales dialect, and the character of the Dales people. He even went as far as translating part of the Bible into the vivid Wensleydale dialect.

65

❶ AISGILL

Where the top of Wensleydale meets the Eden Valley there is a pass crossed by the highest point (1169 ft/356 m) on the Settle–Carlisle Railway. At Aisgill Summit itself there is a fascinating Nature Trail occupying a 5-acre upland field, together with Aisgill Craft Centre. (Open all year daily)

❷ ASKRIGG

Familiar to television viewers as Darrowby, in the BBC series *All Creatures Great and Small*, Askrigg was once celebrated as a clock-making centre. It also had a reputation for hand-knitting, before factory production took over. The church, behind the cobbled market place, is one of the finest in Wensleydale and dates from the early 16th century.

❸ AYSGARTH FALLS

Aysgarth Falls are the most popular waterfalls in the Yorkshire Dales. The River Ure sweeps over a series of three separate falls – the Upper, Mid and Lower Falls – through a narrow limestone gorge.

The Yorkshire Carriage Museum, by the falls, has an outstanding collection of horse-drawn carriages, from the every-day to the lavish. (Open Easter–Oct daily. ♿)

❹ BAINBRIDGE

Bainbridge lies on the River Bain, reputed to be the shortest in England — just 2 miles (3 km) in length. A grassy hillock, just above the village, was the site of the Roman Fort of Virosidium.

During Norman times, Bain-bridge was an administrative centre in the Royal Hunting Forest of Wensley. The old custom of blow-ing the hunting horn every night between Holyrood (September 29th) and Shrove Tuesday to guide travellers off the fells continues to this day. The horn still hangs in the hallway of the Rose and Crown Inn.

❺ CASTLE BOLTON

Castle Bolton is the name of the village which contains Bolton Castle, a massive medieval castle, dating from the 14th century but well preserved. The castle is per-haps most widely famed as the prison which, for a few months in 1568, held Mary Queen of Scots. Refreshments available (Open Mar–Oct daily; Nov–Mar, tours by appointment. Phone 0969 23981) ♿)

❻ COTTERDALE

This cul-de-sac valley below the vast bulk of Shunnor Fell contains just a handful of farms and cot-tages. From here a Corpse Way crosses the fell to Lund's Church. Cotter Force is a small but ex-tremely attractive waterfall on the Cotter Beck. It can be reached just off the main Hawes-Garsdale road by a riverside path.

❼ GAYLE

Gayle lies at the bottom of Fleet Moss, one of the highest and steepest passes in the Pennines, rising up to 1857 feet (566 m) above sea level, up a hill with a 1 in 4 (25 per cent) gradient. The village has an 18th-century water mill, still in use as a saw mill.

❽ HARDRAW FORCE

Fossdale Beck comes down the steep valley of Fossdale to pour over a cliff some 100 feet (30 m) high creating Hardraw Force. It is reputedly the highest single-drop waterfall (above ground) in Britain. A flagged path leads here from the Green Dragon Inn in Hardraw. With care it is possible to walk behind the fall and gaze through the thundering curtain of water.

❾ HAWES

The name Hawes or 't'Haas' means pass. Hawes remained a small community until the 18th century when the Lancaster–Richmond turnpike was completed. Hawes then developed into an important staging post. Several inns were established and on one of them, the White Hart, you can still see the bell that was rung when a stagecoach was about to depart.

The town grew in importance in the 19th century, encouraged by the development of the railway in 1875. It developed an extremely important sheep and cattle market which remains one of the most important in the Pennines. Visit the new Dales Countryside Museum in the former goods shed. There are exhibitions based on rural and household crafts, in-cluding how to make Wensleydale cheese. (Open Apr–Sept, Mon–Sat, Sun afternoon; Oct, Tues, Sat and Sun afternoon. Phone 0969 667494) ⓘ 0969 667450

❿ LEYBURN

Leyburn is the principal market town and administrative centre of the lower part of the dale. The town owes its prominence over rival Middleham to the patronage of the Lords of Bolton who estab-lished the market and the coming of the railway in the 1860s. ⓘ (market square) Phone 0969 23069/22773.

A fine walk from the centre of Leyburn lies along Leyburn Shawl, a wooded ridge to the immediate west of the town, from where there is a spectacular view down the whole of Wensleydale.

⓫ LUND'S CHURCH

This tiny 18th-century chapel in Upper Wensleydale can only be visited on foot, taking the track towards Shaws from the main Kirkby Stephen road.

⓬ SEMERWATER

Semerwater, 2 miles (3 km) from Bainbridge, along the River Bain, is a glacial lake which according to legend was flooded when villagers refused to help an angel disguised as an aged traveller. As retribution the village was flooded in a terrible storm, but church bells can sup-posedly still be heard under the lake waters.

⓭ WEST BURTON

Lying just off the main Bishopdale road, and at the foot of Walden, West Burton is a fine example of a village developed around a large central green. Its distinctive, pyramidal market cross dates from 1820 and recalls a time when a large, weekly market was held on the green. Mill Force waterfall, just behind the northern end of the village, is best viewed from the little packhorse bridge leading to the path onto the fells.

Coverdale and Colsterdale

Preceding page: **Jervaulx Abbey**   **Upper Square, Middleham** (TC)

These two important tributary valleys of the River Ure serve a large and significant area of uplands, where the north-eastern corner of the Dales merges into the Vale of York. Each of these valleys has a distinctive character of its own. Coverdale is a narrow, twisting valley which begins on the shoulders of Great Whernside. It is accessible only from the west by a narrow pass from Kettlewell, Park Rash. The moorland lane passes the Hunter Stone, a medieval, wayside marker post, and, clinging its way to the valley side, the pass hairpins its way into the narrow valley which forms the top end of Coverdale. Once alongside the River Cover the road makes its way past such settlements as Woodale, Horsehouse, Gammersgill and Carlton.

Except, perhaps, on fine summer Sundays when a procession of cars will clog the roads, Coverdale is not a place where you will encounter too many tourists, and for most of the year it is refreshingly quiet.

For those determined to get away from it all, tracks lead over empty moors into Walden, Coverdale and on into Nidderdale. For the most part the tracks run over relatively dry, heather moorland or well-drained peat hags, where apart

Farm gatepost, Coverdale

Lichgate, Coverdale

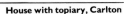

House with topiary, Carlton

from a few sheep and the occasional skylark or kestrel, little is to be seen.

There are few visible remains of the Abbey of Coverham near Cover Bridge, but it was here that the most famous scholar to come out of the eastern dales was educated – Miles Coverdale (1488–1568), Bishop of Exeter and Rector of St Magnus the Martyr, London – but he is best remembered as one of the first translators of the Bible into a version of English the common people could understand.

Middleham, with its magnificent castle prominent on an elevated hillside between the Cover and

Gammersgill

Cottages, Middleham

J Sic labitur Ætas B

CARGRAVE FECIT

17 78

Sundial, Middleham

Middleham Castle (TC)

the Ure, is linked with an even more celebrated but perhaps more enigmatic historical figure, Richard of Gloucester, better known as King Richard III. His savage caricature in Shakespeare's history play is perhaps the most effective character assassination of all time. Far from being a brutal hunchback, the Duke of Gloucester was a shrewd political leader, venerated in the north of England for his generosity and breadth of vision. For a time, in the 1470s, Middleham became the 'Windsor of the North', a centre for fashionable culture and learning, only lapsing into obscurity after Richard's death at Bosworth in 1485. But the Tudors, like all victors, had the privilege of rewriting history, and Shakespeare followed his patrons' example.

Colsterdale, at least in its upper reaches, makes even Coverdale seem crowded. At the top of the valley where a moorland road climbs over to Nidderdale lie the great municipal reservoirs at Leighton and Roundhill, now owned by Yorkshire Water but still serving the citizens of Leeds. They feed the little River Burn, that winds its way through a landscape of tiny hamlets and remote farmsteads, tucked into a deep fold of the hills and attracting only the occasional shepherd and walker.

But a little lower down the dale, as the high moorlands gradually ease their way into fertile, often thickly wooded countryside, a different kind of landscape is prevalent. This is an area of comfortable old farms and scattered villages, of pheasant coverts and lush parkland. Much of this countryside has been shaped by the influence of another remarkable family – the Danbys of Swinton, Barons of Masham, whose enthusiasm for agricultural improvement and landscape gardening knew no bounds.

One member of the family in particular, William Danby, owner of Swinton Park at the turn of the 19th century and a fine scholar and great patron of the arts, carried out many improvements not only to Swinton but in his surrounding estates. His patronage of the impoverished painter Julius Caesar Ibbetson (1759–1817) led Ibbetson to undertake work which now provides a valuable record of rural life in early 19th-century Yorkshire. Another example of his delight in antiquities is the huge stone Druid's Temple, built in the estate woodlands near Ilton in the 1820s. Construction of this folly provided much-needed work for local people. It is a sort of miniature Stonehenge.

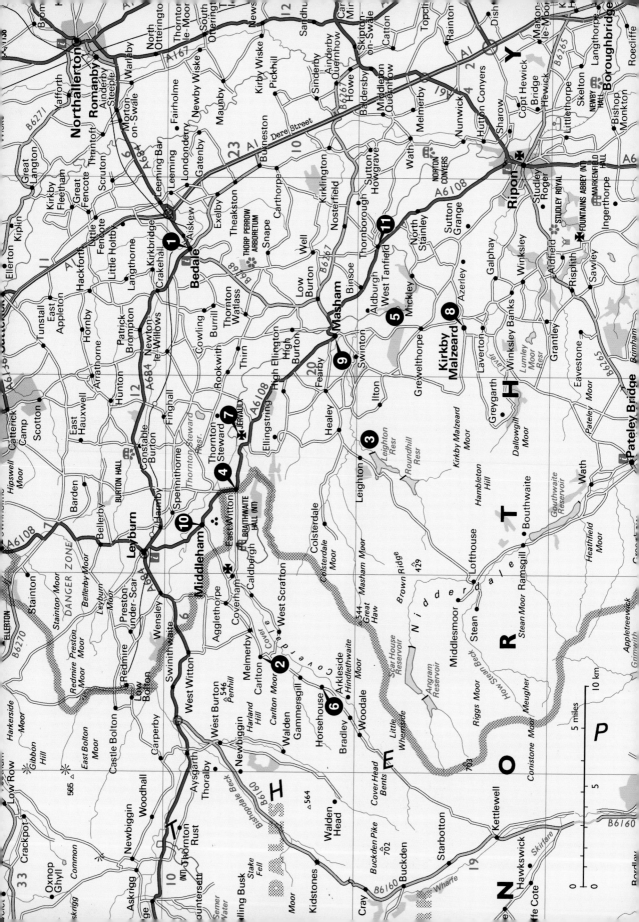

❶ BEDALE

Bedale is an attractive market town, with a wide, partly cobbled main street and an impressive Parish church, St Gregory, much of which dates from the early 14th century. Opposite the church stands Bedale Hall, a building originating in the 17th century, but with extensive 18th-century Palladian extensions which now house the town's museum. Exhibits include a fire engine of 1748, costumes, utensils, old documents and photographs. (Open Spring Bank Hol–Sept daily; Oct–May, Tues. Phone 0677 23131) 🅱 0677 24604.

About 3 miles (5 km) south of Bedale, on the road to Well, lies Thorp Perrow, a remarkable arboretum, with a collection of rare and unusual trees. (Open all year daily)

❷ CARLTON

The largest village in Coverdale, Carlton extends for about a mile along the narrow dale road. The village has many attractive cottages, including one dating from 1667 with an eight-line verse carved above its doorway.

❸ THE DRUID'S TEMPLE

Reached by a signposted, forest road from a point off the Ilton–Healey road, The Druid's Temple is an elaborate folly. It was built in 1805 by William Danby of Swinton. It consists of a series of standing stones, altar rocks, grottos and imitation megaliths in the woods. (Open all year daily)

❹ EAST WITTON

East Witton is another example of a village following a defensive plan around a narrow green. The village was in fact rebuilt in the early 19th century by the Earl of Ailesbury with cottages in plain but attractive local sandstone.

❺ HACKFALL WOODS

At the side of the River Ure, about a mile north-east of the village of Grewelthorpe, lies an area of dense woodland, Hackfall Woods, through which runs a footpath. Though much overgrown, the woods were once cultivated grounds created by a landowner, Mr Lawrence, in the late 18th century, complete with summer houses, grottos, artificial ruins, and 'picturesque' viewpoints looking across the river. The woodlands and walks are in the process of restoration and closed to the public, but can be enjoyed from the public footpath.

❻ HORSEHOUSE

This Coverdale village owes its name to the former trains of pack-ponies that traversed the pass from Wharfedale. It was here that horses and their drivers rested after climbing the pass before continuing to Middleham.

❼ JERVAULX ABBEY

Jervaulx Abbey was founded by a community of monks of the Order of Savigny in 1156, and who later joined the Cistercian Order. The name Jervaulx is Norman-French for Yoredale, and, as well as cheese-making, the monks had a reputation for rearing horses, which may well have laid the foundations for Middleham's long-established connection with the breeding of racehorses. The ruins of the abbey are on private land but are open daily and while the ruins are small compared with Fountains or Bolton, they show the ground plan of a smaller Cistercian house particularly well. They are most attractive in late spring when cascades of purple aubretia cover the grey stonework.

❽ KIRKBY MALZEARD

This large linear village, lies at the centre of a network of lanes, indicating its importance as a market town, having two annual fairs in medieval times. A castle belonging to the powerful Mowbray family once existed here, but it was destroyed by order of King Henry II in 1173. The church, which stands above a little wooded valley, has a Norman doorway with a zigzag-pattern arch and a 15th-century tower.

❾ MASHAM

The old town of Masham has an extensive market place, reflecting the fact that it had a twice yearly toll-free fair and weekly market granted to it by Stephen le Scrope, Lord of Mashamshire in 1393. After World War I it declined in importance, though a lively Wednesday market continues to attract people from surrounding villages. Masham also had an ancient ecclesiastical court of its own to judge offenders of a religious nature, such as non-attendance at church. Known as the Court Peculier (meaning 'particular', the court gave its name to a strong ale – Old Peculier – brewed in the town at Theakston's Brewery.

❿ MIDDLEHAM

Middleham's former links with royalty are reflected in the mighty castle, now owned by English Heritage. It is notable for its keep, one of the largest in England. (Open Apr–Sept daily; Oct–Mar, Tues–Sun. Phone 0969 23899) Middleham itself continued to flourish in the 18th century when it was (and continues to be) a centre for racehorse breeding. It was also an important market town, enjoying a regional reputation for its sheep and cattle fairs, before suffering competition from nearby railway-served Leyburn. Its former commercial importance is indicated from its two market places, three-storey Georgian houses and several handsome inns, which also served a number of important stage-coach routes across the north of England.

⓫ WEST TANFIELD

At West Tanfield a remarkable Tudor gatehouse overlooks the riverside. Known as the Marmion Tower it is open to the public and has a beautiful oriel window. The castle or crenallated manor house of the Marmion family has long gone, but the family effigies survive by their tombs inside the mainly 14th-century church. Chantry Cottage is a delightful Elizabethan cottage with a stone porch.

About 2 miles (3 km) to the east of the village lie the Thornborough Circles, late Neolithic or early Bronze Age earthworks in the form of vast oval circles in the fields, the purpose of which remains a mystery.

Nidderdale

Temple of Piety, Studley Royal

Fountains Hall

Fountains Abbey, Ripon

View over Middlesmoor to Gouthwaite Reservoir

Preceding page: View across Riggs Moor

Farm buildings, Nidderdale

Statue, Studley Royal

Given the haunting beauty and the unspoiled countryside of Upper Nidderdale, many people have asked why this area was not included in the Yorkshire Dales National Park when it was designated in 1954. Paradoxically, this was related, in former years, to its unspoiled nature, being part of the extensive water gathering grounds of Bradford Corporation Waterworks who in late Victorian times and until the 1920s built a series of huge reservoirs to supply the city of Bradford with fresh water. The need to keep water supplies pure limited all building development but it also meant that public access to this area of moorland was strictly limited.

As more liberal policies have emerged in recent years, the top of Nidderdale and the two giant reservoirs of Scar House and Angram, in their desolate, moorland setting, have been increasingly appreciated for quiet recreation. Gouthwaite Reservoir, the earliest to be built, lower down the valley between Wath and Ramsgill is now an important wildlife sanctuary.

But the whole area will now receive increasing protection as part of the Nidderdale Moors Area of Outstanding Natural Beauty which will cover the whole of Upper Nidderdale above Pateley Bridge, and much of Washburndale and the surrounding moorland areas above the valley. It will also include some of the outstanding upper dale villages such as Middlesmoor, Lofthouse and Ramsgill which could otherwise be increasingly vulnerable to development pressures.

This is predominantly a gritstone area, the dale set between high, heather moorlands and peat bog, areas much valued by grouse shooters, but with ample tracks and footpath for walkers and birdwatchers.

On many of the moorland edges there are outcrops of gritstone, often making impressive features in their own right. Brimham Rocks is a good example, one of nature's own sculpture parks where a dramatic combination of large rock outcrops have been weathered by wind, rain and frost to startling effect.

But limestone has a presence here too, most especially at the top end of the dale around How Stean Gorge above Lofthouse where exposures of underlying beds of Carboniferous limestone has produced some impressive riverside formations. In common with other areas of the Dales where limestone and gritstone meet, this is an area of mineral-bearing rocks, and to the east of Pateley

Pateley Bridge

Dam at Scar House

Knaresborough Castle

Bridge rich seams of galena – lead ore – were once worked. It was here the oldest pig of lead was found in the British Isles. Dating from Roman times, it was stamped with the word *Brigantia* indicating its origin in the Roman province that occupied northern England. It is now displayed in Ripley Castle.

Away from the high moorland areas and down river from Pateley Bridge and Summerbridge, the dale begins to soften and broaden, and the villages become more numerous and more densely populated.

Much of this area formed part of the ancient

Royal Hunting Forest of Knaresborough, more accurately described as a hunting reserve of moorland and scrub for such game as red deer and wild boar rather than forest. A local family, the Ingilbys of Ripley, have particular reason to thank the action of one particular wild boar in the Forest, when, in 1355, King Edward III fell defenceless in front of a wild boar while out hunting. The king's life was saved by the prompt action of Thomas de Ingleby who was duly awarded with a knighthood, the use of a wild boar in his crest, a charter to hold a fair and market at Ripley and the cherished freedom to hunt in the

The gorge at Knaresborough

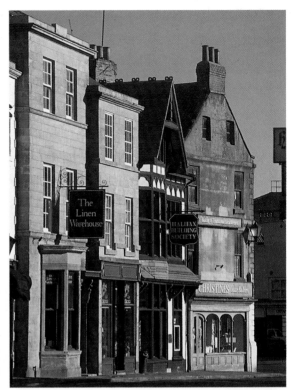

Knaresborough

Brimham Rocks

Royal Forest.

If the ancient town of Knaresborough on the Nidd, with its castle and particular links with King John, provided the focal point for the lower part of Nidderdale, the higher lands between Nidd and Ure, known as Riponshire in medieval times, owed greater allegiance to Ripon, England's smallest cathedral city. Successive generations helped to create the magnificent deer park and landscape garden – including the ruins of Fountains Abbey – at Studley Royal which have earned the ultimate accolade of being chosen as a World Heritage Site by the United Nations.

❶ BIRSTWITH

Birstwith literally means 'barley village'. The barley fields have, however, long since vanished from this pretty estate village. The elegant packhorse bridge was rebuilt in 1822 and has been known as New Bridge ever since.

❷ BRIMHAM ROCKS

The great gritstone outcrops have been weathered by frost, rain and wind into fantastic shapes. Many have fanciful Victorian names such as Idol Rock and the Dancing Bear.

❸ FOUNTAINS ABBEY AND STUDLEY ROYAL

Fountains Abbey, founded in 1132, was one of the richest Cistercian houses in western Europe. The magnificent ruins of Fountains, close by the Renaissance-style Fountains Hall (built with stone from the ruins) and now devoted to an exhibition of the abbey, lie in superb water gardens, once belonging to Studley Hall. The gardens were created in 1720 by the former Chancellor of the Exchequer, John Aislabie. The whole site has been given World Heritage status. (Abbey and gardens open all year daily, except Fri in Jan, Nov and Dec; Fountains Hall open all year daily ♿ ✍)

❹ GOUTHWAITE RESERVOIR

Opened by Bradford Corporation in 1899, the reservoir is linked to Bradford by an immense cross-Dales aqueduct. Gouthwaite village, and the Elizabethan Gouthwaite Hall were demolished and flooded to make way for the reservoir. It is now an important bird sanctuary.

❺ HOW STEAN GORGE

At How Stean the stream forces its way through a narrow limestone gorge which has been opened up to the public by a series of attractive bridges and walkways.

❻ KNARESBOROUGH AND KNARESBOROUGH CASTLE

Knaresborough is one of the oldest and most splendidly situated towns in Yorkshire, lying at the side of a steep gorge of the River Nidd. Its market place with its ancient cross contains what is claimed to be England's oldest chemist's shop, founded in 1256. Other attractions and curiosities include the Cave of the prophetess Mother Shipton, the Petrifying or Dropping Well (a spring which encrusts objects left there with limestone) and a narrow House in the Rock carved into the cliff face. The castle, established in the 12th century, was a favourite venue of King John. (Castle museum open Easter, May Bank Hol–Sept, daily. Phone 0423 869274) ☎ 0423 866886

❼ LOFTHOUSE

Originally a grange established by the monks of Fountains Abbey, this dales village was, for a quarter of a century, the terminus of the Nidderdale Light Railway from Pateley Bridge – the first municipally owned passenger railway in Britain until it closed in 1927.

❽ MIDDLESMOOR

A fine example of a Pennine hill village, built on the end of a high moorland ridge overlooking the dale. Saxon remains in the church suggest the village's ancient origin. From here a track can be followed, with magnificent views, along and over the ridge to Scar House Reservoir.

❾ NEWBY HALL

This Queen Anne house, alongside the River Ure about 4 miles (6 km) from Ripon, is set in exceptional gardens. There is also a superbly decorated 18th- and early 19th-century interior, much of it by Robert Adam at the height of his popularity. The interior includes a mgnificent entrance hall, library, tapestry room with priceless Gobelin tapestries and a sculpture gallery. (Open Apr–Sept, Tues–Sun, Bank Hols; gardens also open Oct weekends. Phone 0423 322583 ♿ ✍)

❿ PATELEY BRIDGE

The principal town in Upper Nidderdale, Pateley Bridge was a former lead-mining town. The excellent Upper Nidderdale Museum, located in the old workhouse just behind the town centre, has exceptional collections of material relating to life in the valley in the last century. It won the Small Museum of the Year Award in 1990. (Open Spring Bank Hol–Sept daily, afternoons only; Oct–Easter, Sun afternoons only; Easter–Spring Bank Hol, weekends only. Phone 0423 711225) ☎ 0423 711147

⓫ RAMSGILL

One of the prettiest villages in the Upper Dale, Ramsgill has an attractive village green overlooked by the ivy-covered Yorke Arms.

⓬ RIPLEY VILLAGE AND CASTLE

Ripley Castle dates back to the 15th century, but was added to over the years, creating a charming mixture of periods and styles. (Open Jun–Sept, Tues–Sun, except Fri; Apr, May and Oct, weekends only. Phone 0423 770152). The village was entirely rebuilt between 1827–8, in a French style.

⓭ RIPON

The massive cathedral, visible from the Pennine foothills, towers above the old town of Ripon. Founded by St Wilfrid in the 7th century, most of the present building dates from between the 13th and 16th centuries, with later restorations. The Anglo-Saxon crypt survives, and can still be seen. St Marygate has the slightly gruesome Ripon Prison and Police Museum, whose collection focuses on law and order from medieval times and the history of punishment and prisons. (Open May–Sept, Tues–Sun, afternoons only. Phone 0756 793706) Wakeman's House Museum (Market Place) has some interesting displays illustrating the town's history. (Open May–Sept, Mon–Sat and Sun afternoon). ☎ 0756 794625

⓮ SCAR HOUSE AND ANGRAM RESERVOIRS

A toll road from just above Lofthouse village leads to the Yorkshire Water Authority Car Park at Scar House reservoir from where it is possible to walk over the reservoir dam and around Scar House reservoir; the path then continues as far as Angram Reservoir below Little Whernside.

Cottage doorway near Otley

Farmhouse near Otley

Statue of Thomas Chippendale, Otley

Preceding page: View across to Blubberhouses Moor

Harrogate has a relatively recent history. Until the 17th century, 'Haregate' as it was known, was just a scatter of cottages on rough common land close to the town of Knaresbrough. It all began in the late 16th century, when Mr William Slingsby was walking his dog and noticed a spring bubbling form the rock. He tasted the waters and as it reminded him of water he had drunk from wells at 'Spaw' in the Belgian Ardennes, he decided to investigate further.

Expert opinion confirmed his view, and in a few years the medicinal value of the spring, known as Tewit Well because of the 'tewits' or peewits often seen nearby, was widely recognized as a cure for almost any ailment – including rheumatism, gout, catarrh, palsy and vertigo.

Other wells were soon discovered nearby, including an especially powerful 'Old Sulphur Well' at a place called Haregate Head, and following the publication of scientific reports over the next few years, bathing-houses, inns and boarding houses were soon being built in numbers near the wells. By the late 18th century Harrogate's fame was established as a fashionable spa, and an elegant town had grown up to serve the needs not only of patients, but of fashionable visitors who

River Wharfe, near Pool

Bridge at Dob Park

Thruscross Reservoir

came to take the waters for the summer season. Harrogate's fame increased in Regency and early Victorian times as the crowned and mitred heads of Britain and Europe came to drink or bathe in the waters.

Handsome new streets and parades were laid out, though much of the ancient common or 'Stray' was happily preserved in the town's centre as a delightful open space. By late Victorian times competition from the famous European spas led Harrogate's enterprising council to develop a 'Kursaal', a splendid hall for concerts and the like, in the tradition of the German spa towns (now the Royal Hall) and the Royal Baths with a variety of new treatments including Turkish baths.

Although the fashion for spa treatments subsequently went into decline, Harrogate successfully changed its image again, this time into an inland resort ('the floral resort') and conference centre; making use of its inheritance of hotels, guest houses and tradition of hospitality, but above all relying on the multi-million pound Conference Centre to attract new kinds of custom.

There is little doubt that Harrogate makes an excellent base to explore the Yorkshire Dales, particularly the eastern side, including its most 87

Cottages at Farnley

Swinsty Reservoir

Drinking fountain at Farnley

Harewood House

The Tewit Well, Harrogate

immediate neighbouring dales of Nidderdale and Washburndale. The Washburn is a tributary of the Wharfe, but like the Nidd has been subject to the activities of reservoir builders, with a series of four reservoirs – Thruscross, Fewston, Swinsty and Lindley Wood, turning an already attractive valley between long ridges of high, heather moorland into what has been described as Yorkshire's Little Lake District, an area where informal recreation in the form of fishing (with a licence), walking and some sailing is almost as important as water gathering.

The old market town of Otley lies just upstream from the confluence of the Washburn with the Wharfe, and is the focal point for the dale. Otley, with its cobbled market place and inns, has kept its character even though it now forms part of the Leeds Metropolitan District. A

Leathley

particular feature of the town is The Chevin, a largely forested ridge which forms a majestic backcloth to the town in the form of the Chevin Forest Park.

The attractive, rolling countryside which separates Harrogate from Washburndale, has many features of its own – the woods and gardens of Harlow Carr, the medieval Haveragh Part with its reservoirs and Almscliffe Crag, a gritstone outcrop which provides a surprisingly good viewpoint into Lower Wharfedale and across to the plain of York, with the White Horse of Kilburn, on the North York Moors, clearly visible when weather conditions are right.

The Yorkshire Dales is one of the 11 officially recognized National Parks in England and Wales. It is an area of incredible beauty and hopefully with the help of organizations such as the National Park Authority will remain so for many years to come.

❶ BLUBBERHOUSES

Little more than a church and a few cottages survive from this Norse settlement which now lies on the main A59 Harrogate–Skipton road. It is located at the head of Fewston Reservoir where a popular car park gives access to good walks.

❷ FEWSTON

Fewston, nestling in woodland close to Swinsty Reservoir, is notable for its charming 17th-century church, in Perpendicular Gothic style. Close by is a parking place and picnic site set in attractive woodland alongside the reservoir. At the far side of the reservoir, in the woods, lies Swinsty Hall, a magnificent Elizabethan yeoman's house, built in 1570; it is a private residence, but clearly visible from the footpath.

❸ HAREWOOD

Home of the Earl of Harewood, cousin of the Queen, Harewood House is one of the finest great houses in the north. It was designed by the York architect, John Carr, probably with the help of Robert Adam, and built in the 1760s, though modifications were undertaken by Sir Charles Barry, architect of the Houses of Parliament, in the 1840s.

Inside there are fine collections of ceramics, and furnishings including much work by Thomas Chippendale, born in nearby Otley. Among the collection of paintings are Italian old masters, English watercolours and some exceptional portraits.

The extensive parkland with lakes, woods and a genuine medieval castle overlooking the hillside were laid out by 'Capability' Brown, and now include extensive, walled, rose gardens, a bird garden and a butterfly house, as well as children's adventure areas, cafeterias and restaurants. (House and gardens open Apr–Oct daily; Feb, Mar and Nov, Sun only. Phone 0532 886213 🅳) Harewood village is a fine example of an estate village, removed from the park grounds to its position outside the main gates in the 1760s.

❹ HARLOW CARR GARDENS

A delightful walk through Harrogate's Valley Gardens, through Harlow Carr Woods leads to Harlow Carr Gardens. Included in the 60 acres of woodland and streamside gardens, are superb displays, as well as an arboretum and glasshouses. Refreshments available (Open all year daily)

❺ HARROGATE TOWN

Harrogate offers much to delight and intrigue the day visitor. There are fashionable shops in Regency parades, an indoor market, coffee houses, wine bars, antique shops and boutiques. You can still hear a string trio playing in the Royal Baths tea room during the summer months. Visit the Royal Pump Room which now forms part of a museum of the spa together with a collection of period costumes. (Open Mon–Sat and Sun afternoon. Phone 0423 503340)

The wide expanses of close-cropped turf on the Stray are bright with crocuses in spring. The Valley Gardens are host to the celebrated Harrogate Spring Flower Show, while other events include an annual International Festival of the Arts, a programme of concerts, an Antiques Show and a host of specialist exhibitions. Harrogate's White Rose Theatre has a regional reputation for lively productions in the setting of a sumptuous Edwardian theatre. ☎ 0423 525669

❻ LEATHLEY

Leathley's church has an early Norman tower, more Saxon than Norman in style. The village enjoys a fine setting, with a central green and a row of 18th-century almshouses.

❼ OTLEY TOWN

A busy, bustling market town on the River Wharfe, Otley's medieval origins are evident from the narrow lanes that radiate off the cobbled market place. The large number of inns were built to satisfy the market-day thirsts of farmers and traders from miles around.

The parish church dates from late Norman times, with an early 14th-century tower. Particularly interesting are the fragments of Anglo-Saxon crosses, the monuments to the Fawkes family of nearby Farnley Hall (related to Guy Fawkes) and the Fairfaxes, famous for their part in the Civil War and, in the portion of churchyard across Church Lane, a gritstone model of Bramhope Railway Tunnel on the Leeds–Harrogate railway. This is a memorial to the many men who died building this impressive line between 1845–9. There are attractive gardens by the riverside below Otley's 17th-century bridge, with boats on the river during the summer months. ☎ (8 Boroughgate) 0943 465151

❽ OTLEY CHEVIN FOREST PARK

If you don't fancy walking to the summit of the 841-foot (256 m) high Chevin, in the Otley Chevin Forest Park, you can let your car do the work and drive up to the car park at Surprise View to enjoy the magnificent panoramic views of Mid Wharfedale and Washburndale.

❾ THRUSCROSS RESERVOIR

When Thruscross Reservoir was constructed by Leeds Corporation, it required not only the damming of the valley but the removal of a hamlet at West End, to a 'new village' which now stands at the crossroads above the reservoir on the Blubberhouses road by the Stone House Inn. The reservoir is now a popular sailing centre and there is also a good choice of easily accessible walks.

❿ TIMBLE

Timble is one of the most delightful and unspoiled villages of Washburndale. Little more than a hamlet of cottages, a Village Institute and Reading Room, but with a busy and welcoming pub, it lies on a quiet back lane even by-passed by the traffic to Fewston.

This is a favourite area for walkers, and a choice of footpaths from Timble lead down to Swinsty Hall and Reservoir. You can also carry on down the riverside to Dob Park, where you will find a single arch packhorse bridge over the River Washburn.

The Settle—Carlisle Railway

Crossing Aisgill Moor

Bridge at Garsdale Head

Signal box, Garsdale Station

Garsdale station

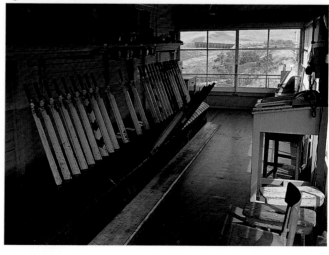

Preceding page: **The Duchess of Hamilton (No 46229) crossing Dent Head Viaduct** (BS)

Described by one leading railway historian as 'The high watermark of Victorian Railway Engineering', the Settle–Carlisle very nearly didn't come about. The origin of the Settle–Carlisle lay in a bitter battle between two rival railway companies to capture the lucrative market that had, over the second half of the 18th century, grown up between the Midlands and Scotland. The battle led to the powerful Midland Railway Company initiating a plan to build their own line through the heart of the Pennines rather than use a line belonging to their rival, the London and North Western Railway and its ill-coordinated connections at Ingleton.

Though the two companies later came to agreement, Parliament forced the Midland Railway to carry on with one of the most ambitious

Railwayman's hut, Aisgill Moor

pieces of railway engineering ever attempted in Britain – a massive main-line standard railway right through the vast mountains between Settle and Carlisle.

The 72-mile (115 km) long railway took seven years to build between 1869 and 1876. As well as costing £3.5 million (a vast sum in the currency values of the time) and requiring the labour of 5000 men, the building work took the lives of well over a hundred men, not only through accidents but also through outbreaks of disease in quite appalling living and working conditions. It was the last major railway to be built almost entirely by manual labour – an achievement comparable to the building of Hadrian's Wall or The Pyramids.

Although it is impossible to ignore the vast cost of the project in terms of both money and men, the final result is a magnificent example of civil engineering and railway architecture, rising to 1169 feet (356 m) above sea level, the highest main line in Britain. It is notable for its many viaducts, the most famous being at Ribblehead.

The Ribblehead Viaduct has an impressive 24 arches, the highest of them 165 feet (50 m) high, but almost equalled by those at Dent Head and Arten Gill.

The many tunnels are also superb feats of engineering, the longest being the 2629-yard (2405 m) long tunnel under Blea Moor.

For many years the Settle–Carlisle line carried Midland and later LMS crack express trains from London, St Pancras to Glasgow and Edinburgh, the most famous being the Thames–Clyde and the Waverley as well as the St Pancras night sleeper. But local trains services to stations such as Horton-in-Ribblesdale, Ribblehead, and Dent (which at just over 1100 ft/335 m above sea level is the highest main line station in England), brought tourists to enjoy the scenic beauty of the area as well as serving the needs of the local communities.

Rationalization of both British Rail's freight and passenger services during the late 1970s and the costs of keeping Ribblehead Viaduct in repair seemed certain to force the closure of the line in the 1980s, but Britain's longest lasting public enquiry against a rail closure, with over 22,000 individual objectors, finally led to a Government decision to abandon the plan and happily the line was saved.

Crucial to its rescue had been the development of a 'Dales Rail' service of regular trains for walkers and visitors to the Dales from local stations, with bus links into the nearby dales. Local authorities followed this initiative by providing enough financial support to pay for the cost of a daily stopping service to meet the needs of local schoolchildren and students, which could also be used by tourists.

The Settle–Carlisle is now one of Britain's most successful scenic railways, with daily services from Leeds, Skipton, Settle and Carlisle, and some from Blackpool and Manchester via Hellifield. There is even an occasional steam-hauled train.

Although many people use the railway purely as a sightseeing trip, others have recognized the value of the line for point-to-point walks between railway stations, leaving a car at Leeds, Skipton or Settle and enjoying a 'car-free' day in magnificent surroundings.

Page numbers in italics indicate a gazetteer entry